REVELATION:
A CHRONOLOGY

BY: DR. JIMMY DEYOUNG

REVELATION: A CHRONOLOGY   DR. JIMMY DEYOUNG

All Scripture references taken from the *King James Version of the Holy Bible.*

Cover design by: Chad W. Smith

REVELATION: A CHRONOLOGY

ISBN - 978-0-557-36265-3

PO Box 2510 Chattanooga, TN 37409

(423) 825-6247

www.prophecytoday.com

Printed in the **United States of America.**

Acknowledgements

Writing a book is not an easy task to accomplish. There are many steps along the way to a finished manuscript and published book. I am grateful to have had a team of people help me along the way and I would like to express my appreciation to them now.

First and foremost I would like to thank my partner in ministry and beautiful wife of over 50 years, Judy. Judy is by my side every day as I am able to travel and speak throughout the world. She is a constant source of wisdom, guidance and inspiration and is integral in every aspect of my life and our ministry.

Next, I would like to thank those who helped with this book from conception to finished product. Thank you to Joy Martin for patiently listening to and transcribing my sermons. To Chad Smith for providing the layout and working through countless formatted versions of the book. To my son, Rick, for reading and re-reading the manuscript and providing editorial suggestions. I would also like to recognize my sister-in-law, Bonnie Varble for her grammatical editing.

Finally, I would like to recognize you the reader. Thank you for recognizing the importance of understanding Bible Prophecy and allowing me to share my ministry with you.

- Jimmy DeYoung

TABLE OF CONTENTS

Revelation: A Chronology

Dr. Jimmy DeYoung

PREFACE

I began to study Bible prophecy in earnest almost 40 years ago. I was working at Word of Life in Schroon Lake, New York, when I was charged with teaching the book of Revelation to campers at the Word of Life Ranch. This task was given to me by the late Jack Wyrtzen (founder and former head of Word of Life). Jack asked me to teach the book of Revelation to campers 13 years of age and under. Needless to say, it was a daunting task. I had to find a way to communicate what seemed, at the time, to be a complicated subject and provide it to these campers in an easy-to-understand format.

Out of this task came my "Revelation Walk-Thru." The Revelation Walk-Thru is a framework that I believe is the easiest way to study and understand the book of Revelation. The Walk-Thru is a study of Revelation based on a timeline of events that are to unfold in the future. I believe that once students of Bible prophecy understand the basics of this timeline, they can then begin to add to their understanding as they continue to study prophetic Scripture. This concept of study is why I named this book, Revelation: A Chronology. This book is a study of Revelation based on a "chronology," which is described in the dictionary as "an arrangement of events in order of occurrence."

This book is a continuing effort on my part to present Bible prophecy in a simple and easy-to-understand format. This book is not meant to be a grand theological dissertation, but a general guide for the layman to the book of Revelation. Many of the subjects I touch on in this book require more in-depth study and for this I encourage you to continue your study in God's Word.

If after reading this book you have questions or comments, I would love to hear from you. Please email me at jimmy@prophecytoday.com. You may also visit my website at www.prophecytoday.com to learn about my ministry and to see a complete listing of the study materials that I recommend.

Note to the Reader:

Welcome to our study of the book of Revelation. God breathed into a man named John the Apostle, the one who would give the message to the seven churches in Asia Minor when he was alive and ministering in that part of the world. These messages were passed along to us today so that we can understand the times in which we are living.

As I mention the Scriptures (many of them will be printed out in this book for you), I hope that you will read them for yourself and not just take my word for it. Reading from your own Bible will reinforce what we are studying together. The more ways and the more times you read the Scriptures, the better you will understand and remember. The same can be said for following along in your Bible when you are listening to any sermon or lesson.

INTRODUCTION TO THE BOOK OF REVELATION

The Three Strands of the Human Family

The Bible tells us in 1 Corinthians 10 that God has made three strands of the human family.

> 1 Corinthians 10:32, *"Give none offence, neither to the Jews, nor to the Gentiles, nor to the church of God."*

For the first 2,000 years of human history (Genesis 1 - 11), there was only one of those strands, the Gentiles, upon the face of the earth. When God created Adam, He created a Gentile. From Adam to Abraham, everyone in the world was a Gentile.

Then in Genesis 12, God calls one of those Gentiles named Abram (who would later become known as Abraham), out of Ur of the Chaldees, down into Canaan and into the Promised Land. He then takes this Gentile and establishes a new strand of the human family, the Jewish people. Abraham was mentioned in Genesis 14 as the first Hebrew; his grandson, Jacob, became the first Israelite (his name changed from Jacob to Israel in Genesis 32); and then his great-grandson Judah would be referred to as a Jew (2 Kings 16:6). So, for the second 2,000 years of human history (Genesis 12 - Acts 1), there were two strands of the human family – Gentiles and Jews.

On the Day of Pentecost, God takes the wall of partition out from between Jews and Gentiles, who had been at enmity with each other (Acts 2; Ephesians 2). With the death, burial, and resurrection of Jesus Christ, God brings Gentiles and Jews together as a new people, one people, a new creation – Christians. And now, for the past 2,000 years, there have been three strands of people: Gentiles, Jews, and Christians.

During the first 2,000 years, there were only Gentiles (Genesis 1-11). During the second 2,000 year period of time (Genesis 12 - Acts 1), there were two strands of the human family, Gentiles and Jews. Now, for the last 2,000 years of human history, we have all three strands of the human family: Gentiles, Jews, and Christians (Acts 2 - Revelation 22).

There are three books in the Bible that cover the timelines for these three strands of the human family. The book of Daniel starts at the Babylonian captivity and takes the history of the Gentiles into Eternity Future. Daniel is a timeline for the Gentiles. The book of Ezekiel also starts at the time of the Babylonian captivity and takes the Jewish people into Eternity Future. God will divide the land that He has promised to give them which is 10 times what they have today (Ezekiel 47-48). Ezekiel is the second timeline for the second strand of the human family, the Jewish people. The book of Revelation starts with the Resurrection of Jesus Christ and takes Christians into Eternity Future. That makes Revelation the timeline for the Christians.

The Proper Title to the Book

Sometimes people mispronounce the title of this book that we are studying. Many times I have people come to me and say, "I love studying Revelations." It is not "Revelations" (plural), it is "Revelation" (singular). It is one Revelation of one Man. Your copy of the Bible may well say, "The Revelation of St. John the Divine." The Apostle John is the one who wrote this book, yet he is not the one who is being revealed. Revelation 1:1 gives the proper title of the book that we are studying.

> Revelation 1:1, *"The Revelation of Jesus Christ, which God gave unto him, to shew unto his servants things which must shortly come to pass; and he sent and signified it by his angel unto his servant John."*

The title of the book is *The Revelation of Jesus Christ*. We will find out that it is going to present the **Person** of Jesus Christ, the **Power** of Jesus Christ, and

13

the **Program** of Jesus Christ. That's the entire Revelation of Jesus Christ in a whole as we look at all 22 chapters.

Let me remind you that this is the last inspired book of the Bible. It is number 66 out of 66 books that 40 men over 1,500 years were inspired to write. God breathed into these men a message He wanted to pass along to each and every one of us. In the New Testament, you have the gospels that open up with the First Coming of Jesus Christ – Matthew, Mark, Luke, and John. And the book of Revelation is dealing with the Second Coming of Jesus Christ. This book is a climax of all the Old Testament and New Testament prophecies. In fact, the book of Revelation will refer to the Old Testament some 350 times. The book of Revelation is the most graphic and detailed on the Second Coming of Jesus Christ. The book of Daniel, which was a timeline for the Gentiles, covers from Daniel until Jesus Christ. The book of Revelation is from Jesus Christ into Eternity Future.

The human author of the book we are studying is John the Apostle. He was a dear friend to Jesus Christ; He traveled those 3½ years while Jesus was in ministry.

This is "The Revelation of Jesus Christ, which God gave unto him" – so God wrote it, and gave it to Jesus – "to shew unto his servants things which must shortly come to pass." And then He – Jesus Christ – would send and signify "it by his angel unto his servant John." So it comes from God, through Jesus Christ, to the an-

14

gel, and ultimately to John the Apostle – John the Revelator, John the pastor of the church at Ephesus.

John ends his life on the Isle of Patmos as a prisoner because of the testimony he has for Jesus Christ. John is the human author of the book. We have other locations in this first chapter that indicate that exact same thing.

> Revelation 1:4a, 9, *"John to the seven churches which are in Asia... I John, who also am your brother, and companion in tribulation, and in the kingdom and patience of Jesus Christ, was in the isle that is called Patmos, for the word of God, and for the testimony of Jesus Christ."*

The Three-Fold Ministry of the Holy Spirit

The Holy Spirit was also involved as He breathed into (the true meaning of inspiration) John the Apostle what to write in this particular prophetic book. There are three ministries of the Holy Spirit in reference to the Word of God.

First, there is Inspiration.

> 2 Timothy 3:16, *"All scripture is given by inspiration of God, and is profitable for doctrine, for reproof, for correction, for instruction in righteousness."*

God breathed into these 40 men over 1,500 years what to write down. Seventeen of these authors in the Old Testament would have a book that they were to write that had prophetic information for us. John the Revelator, of course, would receive the Revelation and

15

pass it along (in the New Testament) to each and every one of us.

Second, there is Revelation. 2 Peter 1:18-21, "a more sure word of prophecy." There Peter exhorts us: if we have this more sure word of prophecy, we would do good to study that prophecy. Also, since "no prophecy of the scripture is of any private interpretation," all prophecy must fit together like a hand in a glove.

And third, there is the ministry of Illumination (John 16). John 16 is recorded during the time in the Upper Room at the Last Supper, the Passover Seder. It took place the night before the Crucifixion of Jesus Christ. Here, Jesus Christ speaks about the fact that He had to go and He was going to send the Spirit of truth – the Holy Spirit – the one who would teach everyone things to come.

> John 16:13, *"Howbeit when he, the Spirit of truth, is come, he will guide you into all truth: for he shall not speak of himself; but whatsoever he shall hear, that shall he speak: and he will shew you things to come."*

Illumination is like walking into a dark room and, with the flip of a switch, flooding the room with light. The room is illuminated, so that you can see everything in the room. The Holy Spirit who wrote the book is not contradictory to himself, but He's complementary to himself, and He will teach us these things to come.

And so you have these three ministries of the Holy Spirit: Inspiration, Revelation, and Illumination. That's the Holy Spirit who wrote the book, who is now living in each and every one of us, and who will assist us in understanding what He is teaching us.

Four Approaches to Interpreting Revelation

There are four apocalyptic books in the Bible: Daniel, Ezekiel, Zechariah, and Revelation. The term "apocalyptic" refers to the use of symbolism to communicate an absolute truth. These symbols are not an allegory or a fairy tale. They are symbols that will be defined or interpreted by another portion of apocalyptic literature some place in the Bible. In fact, that is the rule – in order to interpret apocalyptic literature, that interpretation comes by comparing Scripture with Scripture. It is inductive Bible study and it is the approach that you must take when you are trying to determine what apocalyptic literature is talking about.

In this world today, there are four approaches to interpreting the book of Revelation. There is the non-literal, or allegorical approach to studying God's Word and interpreting the book of Revelation. That's something like a bedtime story, a fairy tale, a legend, a myth, or a fable of something. This is not the way you should approach the interpretation of the prophetic Word of God, the book of Revelation. You should not use an allegorical method of interpretation.

Then there's the Preterist approach. This is talking about the early Church being symbolic of what is going to happen in the book of Revelation. The Preterist would have to say that Revelation was written in 70 A.D. or before 70 A.D., because everything that did happen when the Roman soldiers under General Titus came and destroyed the Temple, devastated the city, and dispersed the Jews to the four corners of the earth was the climax of the book of Revelation. That's why they say it had to be written before those events happened in 70 A.D. The truth is, it was 95 A.D. when the book was written so it is not symbolic of the early Church. Of course, the Preterist approach will deny future events ever taking place.

The third approach to interpreting the book of Revelation is historical. It uses those symbols in the book as pictures of the total Church Age and it then leads up to the Second Coming of Jesus Christ. That means that as you study Revelation you are studying the 2,000-year period of time that we've come to refer to as the Church Age. The problem with this approach to interpreting the book of Revelation is that there is not one Bible teacher who uses that approach who can agree on every single event aligning itself with a prophecy in the book of Revelation. So historically, this is not the approach to take.

What I would suggest as the best approach to interpreting the book of Revelation is the futuristic approach. It looks at the book of Revelation as literal, sensible, and normal. Those are three key words. When you interpret the book of Revelation, you have to believe that it is literal. Remember, apocalyptic literature will use some symbols, but those symbols will be interpreted by another portion of Scripture so you can look at the book of Revelation literally, sensibly, and normally.

It is the premillennial understanding of the book of Revelation – premillennial, of course, meaning that Jesus Christ comes back to the earth before the Millennial Kingdom, Christ's 1,000-year reign on the earth. It is also talking about a pretribulational Rapture of the Church. In Revelation 4:1-2, the Rapture of the Church is pictured. As we study the book of Revelation we will find information that would indicate that the Rapture does indeed take place before the Tribulation begins.

This approach requires a deeper study of a book. One cannot speed read through the book of Revelation and understand what it is talking about. By the way, one cannot go verse by verse through the book of Revelation and fully understand it either. As you approach your study and interpreting the book of Revelation in a literal, sensible, normal way, you have to do it chronologically, not numerically. You cannot go from chapter 1 through the entire book of Revelation to chapter 22, but instead, as we study together this book of Revelation we'll see that it unfolds chronologically and I will go chronologically through the book to help you understand what it taking place.

Remember, in the book of Revelation there are over 350 quotes from the Old Testament. Most of these quotes are from prophetic passages. That, therefore, necessitates that we compare Scripture with Scripture.

Revelation: A Chronology　　　Dr. Jimmy DeYoung

REVELATION: A CHRONOLOGY   DR. JIMMY DEYOUNG

PRELUDE TO THE TRIBU-LATION

A Quick Timeline of the Events of Revelation

In Revelation 1, we see the person and the power of Jesus Christ. The program is going to start and be laid out for us in outline form in chapter 1. Let me share my walk through the book of Revelation.

Chart: A Walk Through Revelation

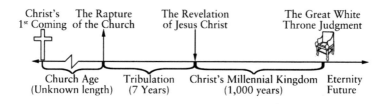

Let me tell you how this book unfolds. The book of Revelation presents Jesus Christ in three areas: His Person, His Power, and His Program. In chapter 1 of the book of Revelation, we see Jesus Christ in his Person and his Power. In chapters 2 and 3, we see Jesus Christ writing a letter to seven churches: seven churches that were alive when John wrote the book in 95 A.D., seven churches that have been alive throughout Church history, and seven churches that are alive today.

In chapter 4, we see the Rapture of the Church. Jesus Christ shouts, the archangel shouts, the trumpet of God sounds, and we are caught up to be with Him in the air. In chapter 5, a great choir of angels singing "Worthy is the Lamb" (Revelation 5:12). In Revelation 6, there is the beginning of three sets of seven judgments. There are Seven Seal Judgments, Seven Trumpet Judgments, and Seven Vial Judgments. In the first 3½ years of the Tribulation Period, the Seven Seal Judgments will take place. Also in the first 3½ years of the Tribulation Period, there will be two witnesses that will preach and 144,000 male virgin Jews will come to know Jesus Christ as Lord and Savior. At the end of these first 3½ years of the Tribulation Period, these two witnesses will be killed. They will lie in the streets of Jerusalem for 3½ days, at which time they will be miraculously raised from the dead and they will enter Heaven. Also at the end of the first 3½ years of the Tribulation Period, there will be a battle in Heaven between the angel Michael, commander in chief of the good angels in Heaven, and Satan and his evil angels. At that point, Satan and his evil angels will be thrown out of Heaven, never to enter Heaven again, they will be cast upon the earth, and they will intensify their persecution with an endeavor to try to destroy all Jewish people across the earth.

In the last 3½ years of the Tribulation Period, the Seven Trumpet and Seven Vial Judgments will take place, culminating with the kings coming out of the east to join the Antichrist to fight the battle of Armageddon. At that point, we Christians who will be in Heaven – having been Raptured up 7 years before this next event, the Second Coming of Christ – will get on white horses along with Jesus Christ and we will come back with Him, back to the Mount of Olives in the city of Jerusalem.

At that point, Satan will be bound for 1,000 years. Christians will rule and reign with Jesus Christ during that same 1,000-year period of time. At the end of the 1,000 years, Satan will be loosed for a season and then he will be captured again by God and thrown into the Lake of Fire. Also at the end of this Millennial Kingdom, there will be the Great White Throne Judgment, at which time Jesus Christ will be the judge. He will sentence those who have rejected Him into the Lake of Fire, which is the second death. After that, Eternity Future: New Heaven, New Earth, and New Jerusalem. That is chronologically how the book of Revelation unfolds.

An Example of Apocalyptic Literature in Scripture

Revelation 1 presents the Person and the Power of Jesus Christ. In Revelation 1:12, we see the Person of Jesus Christ. This is the only portrait that we have of Jesus Christ in word so that we can understand to some extent how He would have looked at his resurrection and in his glorified body

Let me give you the example of how you interpret apocalyptic literature.

> Revelation 1:12, 16a, *"And I turned to see the voice that spake with me. And being turned, I saw seven golden candlesticks;... And he had in his right hand seven stars."*

John talks about the golden candlesticks and the stars. He does not immediately tell us what those symbols mean. But he does later on in the chapter.

> Revelation 1:20, *"The mystery of the seven stars which thou sawest in my right hand, and the seven golden candlesticks. The seven stars are the angels of the seven churches: and the seven candlesticks which thou sawest are the seven churches."*

Here we see Scripture defining Scripture.

The Person of Jesus Christ

We will look at those seven churches in Revelation 2 and 3. They were churches that were actually alive in the day of John the Apostle, the writer of the book of

Revelation. In fact, he was the pastor of the church at Ephesus and most likely was a circuit-riding preacher who had a great ministry among the other six churches as well. But this is simply an example of apocalyptic literature. When he turned, he saw the candlesticks representing those seven churches. The stars that He had in His right hand, will be those angels who minister to these seven churches.

> Revelation 1:13, *"And in the midst of the seven candlesticks one like unto the Son of man, clothed with a garment down to the foot, and girt about the paps with a golden girdle."*

And so we see Jesus Christ standing there. This is what John is able to see and now he's communicating to us what he perceived Jesus Christ to look like.

> Revelation 1:14a, *"His head and his hairs were white like wool, as white as snow; and his eyes were as a flame of fire."*

White hair, as white as snow, depicts the purity and longevity of Jesus Christ. There is much debate to whether Jesus Christ had long hair or short hair. It doesn't say how long or short it was. It says it was white, as white as snow. White in the Word of God depicts purity. "Though your sins be as scarlet, they shall be as white as snow" (Isaiah 1:18). The gray or white head also depicts longevity. Jesus Christ from eternity past through Eternity Future. He never had a beginning, He will never have an ending, He has always been, and He always will be. The white-haired one standing there among the seven churches is the person of Jesus Christ in a resurrected glorified body.

The "flame of fi re" in Jesus' eyes depicts the idea that He has x-ray vision. If you were able to go into a deep word study here you would come to the conclusion that He sees all. As you go through the Word of God, the book of Genesis, the book of Job, the book of Psalms, the book of Hebrews, and other passages in Scripture, you become aware of the fact that the eyes of Christ are upon us at all times. We cannot hide from the view of Jesus Christ. He's looking and watching every single thing that we do. And of course, that's to some extent quite purifying when you realize His eyes are upon our every activity.

Revelation 1:15a, *"And his feet like unto fine brass, as if they burned in a furnace."*

These "feet of fi ne brass" are illustrative of judgment. Jesus Christ is coming back as the judge. He is going to be bringing judgment upon the entire world during a 7-year period of time. This judgment is upon those who have rejected Him as Lord and Savior. It is a judgment upon the satanic trinity – Satan, Antichrist, and False Prophet. It is also judgment upon the Jewish people to turn them to Jesus Christ and judgment upon the Gentile world to bring an end to the times of the Gentiles. That is exactly what is going to happen and these feet, as if they had been burned in the furnace, are depicting judgment.

Revelation 1:15b, *"and his voice as the sound of many waters."*

Have you ever been near Niagara Falls? I was once there with a group of young people. We went out through the tunnel that takes you right under where the water is coming over the top of the falls down to the basin below. It was so loud that I was standing next to a young man, screaming out for him to hear me, but he couldn't. Finally, after I tapped him on the shoulder, he turned and looked at me and was able to make out what I was saying as he read my lips. He could hardly hear me. The voice of Jesus Christ is as the sound of many waters.

His voice, that in a whisper spoke the worlds into existence. His voice, that will shout and call us up to be with Him at the Rapture of the Church. His voice, that in a sweet smooth presence will say, "Well done, thou good and faithful servant" (Matthew 25:21). And then, His voice, that will harshly say, "I never knew you: depart from me, ye that work iniquity" (Matthew 7:23). That is the voice of Jesus Christ, as the sound of many waters.

Revelation 1:16, *"And he had in his right hand seven stars: and out of his mouth went a sharp twoedged sword: and his countenance was as the sun shineth in his strength."*

29

REVELATION: A CHRONOLOGY   DR. JIMMY DEYOUNG

The book of Hebrews talks about the Word of God like a sharp two-edged sword. When He speaks, it is that which cuts. And that voice will speak one day and cast all dead on the battlefield there at Megiddo in the Jezreel Valley, like a two-edged sword.

The "countenance" of Jesus Christ, that means His face. Somebody was concerned about there being no more moon and no more sun. Jesus Christ is going to be the light during Eternity Future. His face as the sun shineth in its very strength.

> Revelation 1:17,"*And when I saw him, I fell at his feet as dead. And he laid his right hand upon me, saying unto me, Fear not; I am the first and the last.*"

The Power of Jesus Christ

Revelation 1:18 presents the Power of Jesus Christ. This is the key verse, a foundation, for all of our understanding of the prophetic Word of God.

> Revelation 1:18, "*I am he that liveth, and was dead; and, behold, I am alive for evermore, Amen; and have the keys of hell and of death.*"

The resurrection of Jesus Christ is the key event in all of history. If Jesus Christ did not die, was not buried, and did not resurrect from the dead, then we are still living in sin and we have no Savior. But, Jesus Christ did die, He was buried, and He did resurrect from the dead.

I had an opportunity to speak to a high school over in West Seneca, New York, near Buffalo. As I was speaking in the assembly, I talked about Jesus Christ, His death, His burial, and His resurrection. After it was all over, a young man came to me and asked me the question, "How did I know that Jesus Christ had resurrected from the dead?"

I said, "It's right here in the Bible."

He said, "You mean you got that out of a Bible?"

I said, "Yes, I did."

He said, "Come on man! You got that out of a book? Were you there when Jesus Christ resurrected?"

I said, "No, I wasn't."

He said, "Do you know anybody who was there when He resurrected?"

I said, "No, I do not."

He thought he had me for a moment, but then I looked him right square in the eye and I said, "Let me ask you a question. Who was the first president of the United States?"

He said, "George Washington, everybody knows that!"

I asked, "Where did you get that from, buddy?"

He said, "It's in every textbook in this high school."

I said, "You mean you got that out of a book? Come on man! Were you alive when George was president?"

He said, "No."

I said, "Do you know anybody who was?"

He said, "No."

We have more evidence to prove that Jesus Christ resurrected from the dead than we have to prove that George Washington was the fi rst president of the United States. The resurrection of Jesus Christ is the key event in all of history. This is the foundation of our faith in eternal life through the person of Jesus Christ. The key event in all of history.

It is also the source of His authority to predict the future. A resurrected Savior, Jesus Christ, is one who with authority can tell us exactly what is going to happen in the future. That's exactly what He does.

Outlining the Book of Revelation

Revelation 1:19, *"Write the things which thou hast seen, and the things which are, and the things which shall be hereafter."*

That gives us a natural outline for Revelation.

I.   Those things which were
     - *Revelation 1*
II. Those things which are
     - *Revelation 2-3*
III. Those things which shall be hereafter
     - *Revelation 4-22*

Let me give you my outline to the study of the book of Revelation. I have three major points.

I.   The Prelude to the Tribulation
     - *Revelation 1:1-4:1*

II. The Program of the Tribulation
   - *Revelation 4:2-19:10*

III. The Postlude to the Tribulation
   - *Revelation 19:11-22:21*

A prelude is what the instrumentalists play as the people are coming in before the church service begins. A postlude is what the instrumentalists play when the church service is over and the people are departing to go their way.

My outline is based on the Tribulation Period, that 7-year time of judgment in the future. It deals with what happens before, during, and after the Tribulation.

Revelation 1 gives us His Person, His Power, and the beginning of His Program. As we continue into chapters 2 and 3, we see the program of Jesus Christ beginning to unfold.

The Seven Churches

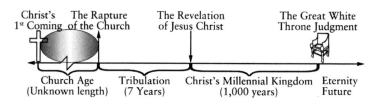

We come to chapters 2 and 3 in the book of Revelation, and this contains the seven letters to the seven churches. John was given these seven messages to give to the churches. Notice what it says in Revelation 1:4: "John to the seven churches which are in Asia."

33

In Revelation 1:11, John is told, *"I am Alpha and Omega, the first and the last: and, What thou seest, write in a book, and send it unto the seven churches which are in Asia; unto Ephesus, and unto Smyrna, and unto Pergamos, and unto Thyatira, and unto Sardis, and unto Philadelphia, and unto Laodicea."*

These seven churches are historical churches. They were churches that were actually alive at the time John wrote the book of Revelation. In fact, John had been the pastor of the church at Ephesus – a church established by the Apostle Paul (Acts 19). After the death of Jesus Christ, John moved to Asia Minor from Israel and he became the pastor of the church at Ephesus. I am sure that he had somewhat of a circuit-riding ministry to the other six churches.

Starting at Ephesus and going to Smyrna, that would be going north along the coast of the Aegean Sea there in what we know as modern-day Turkey, on the western shore of modern-day Turkey. Continuing north beyond that would be Pergamos, and then making a circle around to the church at Thyatira, moving southeast to the church at Sardis, then the church at Philadelphia, coming all the way south to the church at Laodicea, back around then going west over to the church at Ephesus. These were all churches that were alive and well when John wrote the book.

I believe these churches are alive today. I have traveled to the geographical sites of these churches and have visited actual, operating churches in these cities. I have also visited the archaeological remains of several of these churches.

There are characteristics of these churches alive today. As you look at the descriptions of these seven churches and what God has to say about them, they are describing churches that are alive and well on planet earth today. In fact, the descriptions identify individuals in these churches. You can look at seven different Baptist churches and you can see the seven descriptions of the seven churches that were in Asia Minor The individuals in these churches represent seven different types of Christians. I look at the church at Ephesus, for example, and see that they had left their first love. I can point out many churches that have left their fi rst love. Not lost their fi rst love, but walked away from their fi rst love, how it was when they first fell in love with Jesus Christ. And I'm sure that you are aware of the fact that this is applicable for individuals in the church.

There is, to some extent, a look at Church history here as well. These seven churches describe the seven periods of Church history. Now you can't be absolute about this; it is a bit of a stretch to make it work sometimes. But it does give us a glimpse, to some extent, of the seven periods of Church history. So, we see seven churches that were alive when John wrote the book in 95 A.D., and seven churches that are alive today' seven churches that have been alive throughout the last 2,000 years.

Characteristics of Christ

As you study the letters to these seven churches, you are going to fi nd things common to all of the churches. For example, each of the seven messages start with a characteristic of Jesus Christ.

> The church at Ephesus, Revelation 2:1, *"Unto the angel of the church of Ephesus write; These things saith he that holdeth the seven stars in his right hand, who walketh in the midst of the seven golden candlesticks."*

> The church at Smyrna, Revelation 2:8, *"And unto the angel of the church in Smyrna write; These things saith the fi rst and the last, which was dead, and is alive."* (Another characteristic, the risen Jesus Christ speaking to the churches.)

> The church at Pergamos, Revelation 2:12, *"And to the angel of the church in Pergamos write; These things saith he which hath the sharp sword with two edges."*

> The church at Thyatira, Revelation 2:18, *"And unto the angel of the church in Thyatira write; These things saith the Son of God, who hath his eyes like unto a flame of fire, and his feet are like fine brass."*

> The church at Sardis, Revelation 3:1, *"And unto the angel of the church in Sardis write; These things saith he that hath the seven Spirits of God, and the seven stars."*

The church at Philadelphia, Revelation 3:7, *"And to the angel of the church in Philadelphia write; These things saith he that is holy, he that is true, he that hath the key of David, he that openeth, and no man shutteth; and shutteth, and no man openeth."*

The church at Laodicea, Revelation 3:14, *"And unto the angel of the church of the Laodiceans write; These things saith the Amen, the faithful and true witness, the beginning of the creation of God."*

And so, common to all seven messages to the seven churches would be the fact that John is writing about the characteristics of Christ who is the one giving him these messages. In fact, when you stop to think about it, these are the last words of Jesus Christ to the Church. Sometimes we talk about the Pastoral Epistles, which would be 1 and 2 Timothy, to some extent 1 and 2 Thessalonians, and the book of Titus. But that is not the last word to the Church. The last word from Jesus Christ is Revelation chapters 2 and 3, the messages to the seven churches written almost 50 years after those Pastoral Epistles. And so it is, the last word from Jesus Christ is to the seven churches in Asia Minor.

Another commonality to all seven messages is that they are addressed to "the angel of the church." Now this is not the pastor. The word here for angel is "angelos" in the Greek, which means "angel." The Bible tells us that there are angels in these churches and there is an angel in every church. 1 Corinthians 11 talks about angels that will be in attendance when you come to-gether to have the communion service. Angels in every church service. Isn't that awe-inspiring? The reality that God dispatches angels to our church service.

Speaking of angels, the word "angel," or the plural "angels" is used 81 times in the book of Revelation; more times than any other word in the book of Revelation. It talks about evil angels and good angels, and the part they will play in the Second Coming of Jesus Christ. We will get more into that as we continue our study.

"I Know Thy Works"

Let me show you something else that is very inter-esting in our study of these messages to the seven churches. We see that John is going to tell each of the churches that Jesus Christ knows the works of each and every one of them.

> Ephesus, Revelation 2:2, *"I know thy works and thy labour and thy patience..."*

He tells the church at Ephesus He knows what they are doing.

> Smyrna, Revelation 2:9, *"I know thy works, and tribulation, and poverty..."*

He's going to let those in Smyrna know that He is watching. Remember His eyes as a flame of fire, watch-ing all of their activities.

Pergamos, Revelation 2:13, "*I know thy works and where thou dwellest.*"

Thyatira, Revelation 2:19, "*I know thy works, and charity, and service, and faith, and patience, and thy works....*"

Sardis, Revelation 3:1, "*...I know thy works, that thou hast a name that thou livest, and art dead.*"

That is a shocking statement that Jesus said about the works of the church at Sardis.

Philadelphia, Revelation 3:8, "*I know thy works....*"

Jesus has some very positive statements to make about the church at Philadelphia.

Laodicea, Revelation 3:15, "*I know thy works, that thou art neither cold nor hot....*"

Jesus tells what is going to be the result of that. He will spew them out of his mouth.

He gives an exhortation to all of the churches. Since He knows the works of each and every church, He's going to tell them, I want you to make certain you do what I've called you to do. These are the last words of Jesus Christ not only to the churches but also to the church members, the exhortations found within them will be such a blessing, and it will be a great personal Bible study.

He that hath an ear...

He makes a promise in all of these messages to these seven churches. He says in every single one of them: *"He that hath an ear, let him hear."* Go back to chapter 2 and let's start with the church at Ephesus. He makes that statement in verse 7: *"He that hath an ear, let him hear what the Spirit saith unto the churches."*

Then common also in all the messages is: *"to them that overcometh."*

> 1 John 5:4-5, *"For whatsoever is born of God overcometh the world: and this is the victory that overcometh the world, even our faith. Who is he that overcometh the world, but he that believeth that Jesus is the Son of God?"*

Overcomers, then, are those of us who know Jesus Christ as our Lord and Savior. He is talking to the saved members of the churches. He is talking to you; if you have an ear, listen and hear what is going to be given to those that overcome.

He makes a promise to those who are overcomers. Here in verse 7, to the church at Ephesus, He says, "To him that overcometh will I give to eat of the tree of life, which is in the midst of the paradise of God." "Paradise of God" could be translated "garden" as well. And so that's talking about during the Millennial Kingdom; the tree of life will be there in the city of Jerusalem, and we will be able to eat the fruit from that tree of life. A similar phrase – "To him that overcometh" – is mentioned in all seven messages.

Trace through these seven messages and notice the phrase "I know thy works;" which is followed by an exhortation for each church. There is commendation for all of the churches except one. The commendation goes to every church except the church at Laodicea, and He condemns the church at Laodicea. There is also somewhat of a condemnation against all of the churches except Smyrna and Philadelphia. He has no negative statements to say about these two churches. So this is a part of the structure of the letters to the seven churches in the book of Revelation, chapters 2 and 3.

To the Overcomers

The Lord says if you are an overcomer, listen to what I have to say. He makes this statement to the members of the church at Smyrna. He tells them what He is going to do. But those who are in Jesus Christ, those who are overcomers, He tells them that they shall not be hurt of the second death. That's verse 11 in the message to the church at Smyrna.

> Pergamos, Revelation 2:17, "...To *him that overcometh will I give to eat of the hidden manna, and will give him a white stone, and in the stone a new name written, which no man knoweth saving he that receiveth it.*"

This is so exciting as we think about those things that He has promised to those who are overcomers,

41

those who are believers in each of the churches. At Thyatira He makes the same statement.

> Thyatira, Revelation 2:26-27, *"And he that overcometh, and keepeth my works unto the end, to him will I give power over the nations: And he shall rule them with a rod of iron; as the vessels of a potter shall they be broken to shivers: even as I received of my Father."*

Everyone that has an ear, listen up to what is said to the seven churches.

> Sardis, Revelation 3:5, *"He that overcometh, the same shall be clothed in white raiment; and I will not blot out his name out of the book of life, but I will confess his name before my Father, and before his angels."*

You will not have your name blotted out of the Book of Life if you know Jesus Christ as Lord and Savior. I do not think that you can lose your salvation. In fact, from studying God's Word, there is no way, once you have come to know Jesus Christ as Lord and Savior, that you can lose your salvation.

It seems to say in this passage that your name will not be blotted out of the Book of Life. In other words, it had to be in the Book of Life, so it won't be blotted out. Is that talking about the fact that when you get saved your name is put in the Book of Life? No, I think it's saying that the names of everyone ever brought into this world, their names were in the Book of Life in eternity past, and Jesus Christ said, if you are an over-

42

comer, if you come to know Jesus as your Lord and Savior, I will not blot your name out of the Book of Life.

He's done everything possible to bring us to Him to have fellowship with Him. Christ has put our names in the Book of Life in eternity past in anticipation of us trusting Him as Lord and Savior and coming to the Father through the Son, Jesus Christ. What a blessing that is!

> Philadelphia, Revelation 3:12, *"Him that overcometh will I make a pillar in the temple of my God, and he shall go no more out: and I will write upon him the name of my God, and the name of the city of my God, which is new Jerusalem, which cometh down out of heaven from my God: and I will write upon him my new name."*

Though the church at Laodicea was condemned, to him that overcometh God is going to give him something as well.

> Laodicea, Revelation 3:21-22, *"To him that overcometh will I grant to sit with me in my throne, even as I also overcame, and am set down with my Father in his throne. He that hath an ear, let him hear what the Spirit saith unto the churches."*

The Rapture of the Church

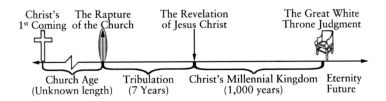

Revelation 4:1 concludes the prelude to the Tribulation; verse 2 begins the 16-chapter description of the 7-year period of time called the Tribulation. In chapter 4 and verse 1 we see John is going to change his location from the earth to Heaven. Jesus Christ continues to show him all that will take place through the angel who is giving the message to John so he can write it down.

> Revelation 4:1a, *"After this I looked, and, behold, a door was opened in heaven: and the first voice which I heard was as it were of a trumpet..."*

That phrase, "as it were," is used 52 times in the book of Revelation. What it actually means is "it seems to be, but not really is." In other words, it seems like it was a voice of a trumpet, but it was not really the voice of a trumpet.

> Revelation 4:1b, *"talking with me; which said, Come up hither, and I will shew thee things which must be hereafter."*

That's an interesting phrase, "Come up hither." We'll see in chapter 11, that is the same phrase that is used to call the two witnesses into Heaven. And it may well be what Jesus Christ will shout at the Rapture, "Come up hither!" Now, I don't have any dogmatic stand on that, but it seems like a good candidate for what he will shout to call us up to be with him.

Before we look at the details of the coming Tribulation, please notice the last phrase of Revelation 4:1. It says "And I will shew thee things which must be hereafter." This phrase declares that the rapture takes place and then the things which must happen (the seven years of Tribulation) will follow.

Revelation 4:2, *"And immediately I was in the spirit: and, behold, a throne was set in heaven, and one sat on the throne."*

This is John speaking. He moves from the earth to the throne room in Heaven. This is depicting the Rapture of the Church. In the study of the book of Revelation, I place the Rapture of the Church between Revelation 4:1 and 4:2.

The procedure is laid out in 1 Thessalonians 4:13-18. Now we discussed this earlier when we studied about the main events in the future, the Rapture being one of them. What will happen is that Jesus Christ is going to shout...

1 Thessalonians 4:16, *"For the Lord himself shall descend from heaven with a shout, with*

*the voice of the archangel, and with the trump
of God: and the dead in Christ shall rise first."*

Those who have already died knowing Jesus Christ
as their Lord and Savior will be somewhere on this
earth. They may be in a grave somewhere, they may be
in the middle of the ocean because of a drowning, they
may have burned up in a fire and their ashes scattered,
we don't know exactly where they are going to be, but
Jesus Christ, who brought them all into existence, will
gather them.

> 1 Thessalonians 4:17, *"Then we which are alive
> and remain shall be caught up together with
> them in the clouds, to meet the Lord in the air:
> and so shall we ever be with the Lord."*

Let me remind you, the English word "rapture" is
not used in the Bible. The Latin verb "rapturo" is
where we get the word for rapture. The tense "rapie-
mur" (the first person plural future indicative passive
tense, to be exact) is used in the Latin Vulgate in this
verse. We will be caught up – Raptured – to meet Him
in the air.

Jesus Christ had referred to the Rapture of the
Church in the upper room during the Passover Seder
that evening just before He would be crucified the next
afternoon at 3:00 pm. As recorded in the Gospel of
John, He said,

> John 14:1-3, *"Let not your heart be troubled: ye
> believe in God, believe also in me. In my Fa-
> ther's house are many mansions: if it were not*

so, I would have told you. I go to prepare a place for you. And if I go and prepare a place for you, I will come again, and receive you unto myself; that where I am, there ye may be also."

The Second Coming of Jesus Christ, which is different than the Rapture, is when Jesus Christ comes back to the earth. We will be following him on white horses, stepping down on the Mount of Olives in the city of Jerusalem. But notice the phrase in John 14 where he says, "I will ... receive you unto myself." That is Jesus Christ calling us up to join Him in Heaven and, 7 years later, we will return to the earth with Him. The Rapture of the Church is the next main event in God's calendar of activities.

Reasons for the Tribulation

There are several reasons for the Tribulation Period. These reasons will give us an understanding as to why we as Christians will not be included in that 7-year Tribulation Period, but taken out at the Rapture of the Church before the Tribulation begins.

1. These 7 years are going to be a time of evangelization of the Jewish people. When we study about the two witnesses, we'll see that 144,000 male virgin Jews will come to know Christ as Lord and Savior and then travel the world telling people the gospel of the kingdom so they may have opportunity to receive Jesus Christ. This will be a great time of evangelism.

2. It is a time to bring an end to Gentile world powers. In Daniel, the prophet describes two visions of the major Gentile world powers, and their ultimate end. They will be replaced by Jesus Christ coming back to establish his kingdom, thus bringing an end to the Gentile world powers.

3. It is a time to bring about the defeat of the satanic trinity: Satan, the Antichrist, and the False Prophet. Satan trying to be the replica of God the Father, the Antichrist copying Jesus Christ the Son, and the False Prophet endeavoring to be the reproduction of the Holy Spirit. These three will be defeated at the end of the Tribulation Period, and the Antichrist and the False Prophet will be thrown into the Lake of Fire. Satan will be cast into the Bottomless Pit for 1,000 years and then he ultimately also will be thrown into the Lake of Fire.

Will Christians be in the Tribulation?

Christians will not be on the earth during this Tribulation Period. Remember, the Rapture takes place before the Tribulation. Notice again Revelation 4:1b *"...and I will shew thee things that must happen hereafter."* Revelation 4:2 through Revelation 19:11 (almost 16 chapters) details what must happen after the rapture.

There is also the promise made by Jesus Christ to the church at Philadelphia.

> Revelation 3:10, *"Because thou hast kept the word of my patience, I also will keep thee from the hour of temptation, which shall come upon all the world, to try them that dwell upon the earth."*

The "hour of temptation" is referring to the Tribulation Period, and I want you to notice what Jesus said he will do: "I … will keep thee from." Not "take thee out of," but "keep thee from" that Tribulation Period. That is great evidence that we, as Christians, will not be a part of the Tribulation Period.

The Church is referred to 25 times in the book of Revelation. It is referred to 19 times before Revelation 4:1, and 6 times after Revelation 19:11. Now check back with our outline for the book of Revelation. That means during those 16 chapters describing the Tribulation Period, the word "church" is not used at all. Zero percent of the time that the Church is referenced in the book of Revelation is during those 16 chapters describing the Tribulation Period.

Israel is referred to 30 times in the book of Revelation:. 3 times before Revelation 4:1, 1 time after Revelation 19:11, and 26 times – 86 percent of the time – in those 16 chapters describing the Tribulation Period.

There are additional reasons that Christians will not be in the Tribulation Period. Remember Daniel's prophecy of 70 weeks, or 490 years? The first 483

49

years, or the first 69 of the 70 weeks, the Church was not in that period of time. Thus, the last 7 years, as found in Daniel 9:27, the 70th week of Daniel, will not have the Church in it either. So that means that we will not be a part of the Tribulation Period. We will be taken out from this world before the Tribulation Period. Jesus promised, "I ... will keep you from" the Tribulation Period (Revelation 3:10).

The Rapture of the Church is the next main event on God's calendar of activities taking place in the very near future. There is no prophecy that has to be fulfilled before the Rapture of the Church takes place – not one. The Rapture of the Church will actually initiate the rest of history and what is going to happen prophetically, according to God's Word. So all prophecies that are yet to be fulfilled take place after the Rapture of the Church.

Christians during the Tribulation

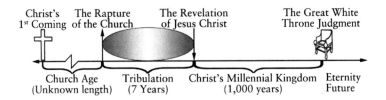

Christ's 1ˢᵗ Coming	The Rapture of the Church	The Revelation of Jesus Christ	The Great White Throne Judgment
Church Age (Unknown length)	Tribulation (7 Years)	Christ's Millennial Kingdom (1,000 years)	Eternity Future

The Judgment Seat of Christ

What happens when the Rapture has taken place? Immediately, we stand before Jesus Christ, never to leave his presence again (1 Thessalonians 4:17). We will be face to face with Jesus. At that point in time, the Judgment Seat of Christ will take place.

The Judgment Seat of Christ is to determine what rewards we receive, what crowns Jesus Christ will give us for those things that we have done in His power and for His glory. It will also be a time of loss, the loss of reward because we did many things in our own power and for our own glory.

Romans 14:10 and 2 Corinthians 5:10 both say that each of us who know Jesus Christ as Lord and Savior must stand before Him for the Judgment Seat of Christ.

> 1 Corinthians 3:12-15, "*Now if any man build upon this foundation gold, silver, precious stones, wood, hay, stubble; Every man's work shall be made manifest: for the day shall declare it, because it shall be revealed by fire; and the fire shall try every man's work of what sort it is. If any man's work abide which he hath built thereupon, he shall receive a reward. If any man's work shall be burned, he shall suffer loss: but he himself shall be saved; yet so as by fire.*"

What actually takes place here at the Judgment Seat of Christ? We stand before him and all of the works that we have done in the past are going to be judged. We shall receive rewards for those works we did in His power and for His glory. Those will be the "gold, silver and precious stones" works. Those works we do in our power for our own glory – and sadly I have to admit that many works I have done, I'm sure, were in that

51

category – they will be the "wood, hay and stubble" works. They will be burned up and I will receive no reward for those particular works.

It's like taking a balance and on one side of the balance you have the gold, silver, and precious stones works, those works done for His glory and His power; and the wood, hay, and stubble works, those works done by us for our own glory, are dropped into the fire. When the fire touches gold, silver, and precious stones, it simply purifies it. When it touches wood, hay, and stubble, it consumes it. The balance is come up out of the fire; the only works remaining are those gold, silver, and precious stones works. Those are the works for which we shall receive a reward.

The Rewards at the Judgment Seat

As we realize the awesome truth that we are each individually going to stand one day before the Almighty Judge at the Judgment Seat of Christ, we should think about the five crowns that we are eligible to receive.

> The Crown Incorruptible, 1 Corinthians 9:25-27, "*And every man that striveth for the mastery is temperate in all things. Now they do it to obtain a corruptible crown; but we an incorruptible. I therefore so run, not as uncertainly; so fight I, not as one that beateth the air: But I keep under my body, and bring it into subjection: lest that by any means, when I have*

preached to others, I myself should be a castaway."

The Incorruptible Crown for bringing our bodies under subjection, that is to say, controlling and not giving into the lusts of the flesh.

The Crown of Rejoicing, 1 Thessalonians 2:19, *"For what is our hope, or joy, or crown of rejoicing? Are not even ye in the presence of our Lord Jesus Christ at his coming?"*

To whom is Paul writing? He is writing to the people at Thessalonica. People that he, just three weeks before he wrote this letter, had led to Jesus Christ as their Lord and Savior. They would be standing with him at the coming of Jesus Christ. So this Crown of Rejoicing is for being a soul winner.

The Crown of Life, James 1:12, *"Blessed is the man that endureth temptation: for when he is tried, he shall receive the crown of life, which the Lord hath promised to them that love him."*

The Crown of Life is for those who endure temptation. Temptation is not sin; it's yielding to temptation that becomes sin. You are able to stand temptation, thus, you are able to receive the Crown of Life.

The Crown of Glory, 1 Peter 5:1-4, *"The elders which are among you I exhort, who am also an elder, and a witness of the sufferings of Christ, and also a partaker of the glory that shall be revealed: Feed the flock of God which is among you, taking the oversight thereof, not by con-*

53

straint, but willingly; not for filthy lucre, but of a ready mind; Neither as being lords over God's heritage, but being ensamples to the flock. And when the chief Shepherd shall appear, ye shall receive a crown of glory that fadeth not away."

The Crown of Glory is for those of us who feed the flock, those who help Christians mature in their lives.

The Crown of Righteousness, 2 Timothy 4:8, *"Henceforth there is laid up for me a crown of righteousness, which the Lord, the righteous judge, shall give me at that day: and not to me only, but unto all them also that love his appearing."*

Among the last statements of the Apostle Paul includes those written to young Timothy concerning the Crown of Righteousness. I love this passage of Scripture. In 2 Timothy 4, Paul talks about running the race, fighting the fight, and keeping the faith. The crown of righteousness is for all of us who anticipate with great eagerness – who love the appearing of Jesus Christ.

Revelation 4:10-11, *"The four and twenty elders fall down before him that sat on the throne, and worship him that liveth for ever and ever, and cast their crowns before the throne, saying, Thou art worthy, O Lord, to receive glory and honour and power: for thou hast created all things, and for thy pleasure they are and were created."*

And so, after this Judgment Seat of Christ, after we have received the crowns we shall receive, we are going to cast them at the feet of Jesus Christ in thanksgiving for what he has done for us (Revelation 4:10). The Apostle Paul in 2 Corinthians 5 said he was ambitious to receive as many crowns as possible, not to build his ego, but to be able to cast them at the feet of Jesus Christ in thanksgiving for what He has done for us.

Chart: The Five Crowns for Faithfulness

Reward	For	Text
Crown Incorruptible	Bringing our bodies under subjection	1 Corinthians 9:25-27
Crown of Rejoicing	Being a soul winner	1 Thessalonians 2:19
Crown of Life	Enduring temptation	James 1:12
Crown of Glory	Feeding the flock	1 Peter 5:1-4
Crown of Righteousness	Loving Christ's appearing	2 Timothy 4:8

The Marriage of the Lamb

There is a period of time after the Rapture of the Church and before the Tribulation begins. In Daniel 7, we see that the 10 horns appear, the Revived Roman Empire coming into existence. Out of the 10 horns, the little horn will arise. "Little horn" is one of 27 names for the Antichrist. He is going to confirm a peace treaty between the Jewish people and their enemies (Daniel 9:27). Those three events have to happen between the time of the Rapture of the Church and the beginning of the 7-year Tribulation Period. Actually, the confirmation of that peace treaty by the Antichrist with the Jewish people and their enemies will start the clock ticking on those 7 years.

> Revelation 19:7, "*Let us be glad and rejoice, and give honour to him: for the marriage of the Lamb is come, and his wife hath made herself ready.*"

The Marriage of the Lamb should not be confused with the Marriage Supper of the Lamb. There are three parts to a Jewish marriage: the engagement or the betrothal period, the wedding ceremony itself, and a multi-day wedding feast.

The fathers of the bride-to-be and the groom-to-be will meet with the two young people, the bride-to-be and the groom-to-be, and the fathers will agree that it would be okay for these two families to be joined together and this young couple to come to know each other as husband and wife. That is the engagement period.

After the agreement is settled, the groom-to-be says to his bride-to-be, "I have to go back to my father's house and I am going to add an addition to my father's house for us to live in. It will be our home in the beginning of our marriage. I'm not sure how long it's going to be before I have finished preparing our place for us to live, but you go back home and you get your wedding gown all ready because when I get ready, I'll come quickly to gather you up, we will go to the rabbi and he will perform the wedding ceremony. We shall then be joined together as husband and wife."

The groom-to-be then returns to his father's house. If it were up to him when he was going to have everything ready for his new bride, he would probably put up a lean-to and say, "Listen, I'm ready, this is all set for us to live in!" And he would rush back to get his bride. But the truth, is the groom-to-be has to wait until his father gives word that he indeed has prepared a place that is suitable for the new young couple to live in.

Once the father is satisfied with the dwelling place, he tells his son, "Go get your bride!"

At that point in time, the groom-to-be will call his best man who will go through the streets on the way to the bride-to-be's home, shouting, "Behold the bridegroom cometh!" They will come together and the ceremony will take place before the rabbi and a few select guests who will join to witness the wedding ceremony.

After the wedding ceremony has been completed, the new bride and the new groom will go into a secret, secluded place, and they will consummate the marriage.

The friends and family of the new couple have then gathered for the celebration; the couple returns, and the party can begin. The wedding feast lasts for 7 days. I've been to one of those 7-day feasts, actually I showed up on the fifth day and everything was still going strong. They were celebrating this young couple who had been joined together as husband and wife.

Do you see the connection between Christ and the Church and the Jewish wedding – the engagement, the wedding ceremony, and the wedding feast? We are in the engagement period right now. Remember, Jesus promised in John 14 to go to His Father's house and prepare a place for us. One of these days, God the Father will tell Jesus, "Go get your bride!" and Jesus will come back to gather the Church – the body of Christ, the bride of Christ – to be His new bride and the marriage will take place.

We are now to be preparing our wedding gowns, the white robes of Revelation 19:8. Our righteous acts that will be tried by fire at the Judgment Seat of Christ is what prepares those robes. Every single act that you did in His power and for His glory, will make up that beautiful wedding gown as you stand before your new groom, Jesus Christ. Then the wedding feast, the Marriage Supper of the Lamb, will take place. It will take place in Heaven during those 7 years of terrible Tribulation upon the face of the earth.

REVELATION: A CHRONOLOGY   DR. JIMMY DEYOUNG

REVELATION: A CHRONOLOGY   DR. JIMMY DEYOUNG

THE PROGRAM OF THE TRIBULATION

Revelation 5 explains what unfolds after the Marriage of the Lamb has taken place in Heaven. Remember, we are studying the book of Revelation chronologically. So far, we have been going somewhat numerically through the book of Revelation, but you'll never understand Revelation if you study it numerically (chapters 1 through 22). You have to study it chronologically, and from here on out, that will be different than going chapter by chapter.

The Antichrist (First Seal Judgment)

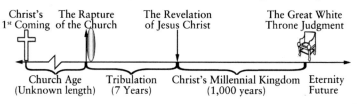

Revelation 5:1, *"And I saw in the right hand of him that sat on the throne a book written within and on the backside, sealed with seven seals."*

This is the seven-sealed book of judgment and it's the title deed to the earth.

Let me clarify what I mean when I say "title deed to the earth." Ultimately, God will give dominion of the earth to His Son Jesus Christ (Daniel 7:13-14). Before the Lord gives Him that kingdom, the earth and earth dwellers must be brought under submission. God will use these sealed judgments to bring them under submission. The sealed book is what is needed for this dominion to be fulfilled, therefore, it is the title deed to the earth.

The seven-sealed book of judgment is not like the book that you hold in your hand now. But instead it would be a scroll. In the time that the book of Revelation was written (95 A.D.), when they referred to a book it was a reference to either two rolls of a scroll that came together or one roll. Most of the time, if it was a single roll, they would use a wax-type seal to secure the closed book, so that it would not unfold too quickly when opened. The book in Revelation 5 has seven of those seals on it.

A problem arises. Who is qualified? Who should be the one to open this sealed book? John becomes upset thinking that none is worthy – but he is reassured that there is One that is worthy to open the book.

Revelation 5:2-5, *"And I saw a strong angel proclaiming with a loud voice, Who is worthy to open the book, and to loose the seals thereof? And no man in heaven, nor in earth, neither under the earth, was able to open the book, neither to look thereon. And I wept much, because no man was found worthy to open and to read the book, neither to look thereon. And one of the elders saith unto me, Weep not: behold, the Lion of the tribe of Juda, the Root of David, hath prevailed to open the book, and to loose the seven seals thereof."*

Jesus takes the sealed book out of the hand of God the Father, and He then has the "title deed to the earth."

The Seven Seal Judgments

God is going to give His Son, Jesus Christ, dominion over all of creation. That dominion will be in a kingdom that will be established and located in the city of Jerusalem. Jesus Christ will sit upon His throne in the Holy of Holies on the Temple Mount in the Temple that He Himself is going to build.

This "title deed to the earth" is also the sealed book that is going to be opened up and from which the Seven Seal Judgments are going to be released. Earlier in our walk through the book of Revelation we said these Seven Seal Judgments take place in the first 3½ years of the Tribulation Period. There are three sets of seven judgments each: the Seven Seal Judgments, the Seven Trumpet Judgments and the Seven Vial Judgments; twenty-one judgments in all, that get progressively worse as you go through the book of Revelation.

During the first 3½ years of the Tribulation Period, these Seven Seal Judgments will take place. In Revelation 6:1, we see the beginning of these judgments that will be released upon the earth.

The First Seal Judgment – the Antichrist

Revelation 6:1, *"And I saw when the Lamb opened one of the seals, and I heard, as it were the noise of thunder, one of the four beasts saying, Come and see."*

The Lamb is Jesus Christ. Thus, the pronoun "he" in verses 3, 5, 7, 9, and 12 – he who opens the seals– refers back to the Lamb, Jesus Christ. Jesus Christ Himself will be the One who will release these sealed judgments upon the earth.

Revelation 6:2, *"And I saw, and behold a white horse: and he that sat on him had a bow; and a crown was given unto him: and he went forth conquering, and to conquer."*

This one comes on a white horse. Many people jump to the conclusion that this must be Jesus Christ, and He's coming on a white horse. Jesus Christ is indeed coming on a white horse (Revelation 19), but He comes at the end of the Tribulation.

However, the events of Revelation 6 occur at the beginning of the Tribulation. This is soon after the Rapture of the Church has taken place. This is the beginning of that 7-year period of time, all of these seal judgments will be released during the first 3½ years of the Tribulation. So this person on the white horse cannot be Jesus Christ.

Remember, the satanic trinity tries to replicate the Holy Trinity: Satan the equivalent of God the Father, the False Prophet the equivalent of the Holy Spirit, thus the Antichrist is the equivalent of Jesus Christ the Son. And so this one who comes on a white horse, trying to be like Jesus Christ, is the Antichrist. Notice he has a crown on his head and he has a bow in his hand with no arrows. That means he comes and establishes peace.

Daniel 9:27 deals with the Antichrist who comes on the scene and says that he will establish a peace between the Jews and their enemies for a period of time. That actually begins the clock ticking on the 7-year Tribulation Period. I happen to believe that the Antichrist is alive and well on planet earth today.

In Daniel 7, the Antichrist is referred to as the little horn. The little horn that comes out of the 10 horns, referring to the fact that he comes out of that last of the Gentile world powers, the Revived Roman Empire. That gives us evidence that he is going to be a Gentile. The Antichrist, who is going to be the false messiah, is not going to be Jewish. The question will probably come up – Why in the world would the Jewish people believe that a Gentile is the Messiah?

2 Thessalonians 2:8-12 talks about those who have rejected the love of the truth. This means they are rejecting the gospel that they might be saved. Jesus Christ Himself will send a strong delusion and cause those who have rejected Him to believe the lie of the Antichrist. There will be many Jews who will come to know Christ as Lord and Savior; a great number of them. But the truth is, there will be those who reject Jesus Christ and they will believe the lie because of their rejection. That is what God says through the writings of the Apostle Paul. They that have rejected the love of the truth that they might be saved. God shall send them a strong delusion so that they believe the lie.

> Daniel 11:36-38, *"And the king shall do according to his will; and he shall exalt himself, and magnify himself above every god, and shall speak marvellous things against the God of gods, and shall prosper till the indignation be accomplished: for that that is determined shall be done. Neither shall he regard the God of his fathers, nor the desire of women, nor regard any god: for he shall magnify himself above all. But in his estate shall he honour the God of forces: and a god whom his fathers knew not shall he honour with gold, and silver, and with precious stones, and pleasant things."*

Daniel 11:36-45 describes the Antichrist's activities and attitudes. In verse 36 we see another of the names for the Antichrist, the "willful king." He will do as he wants to do. He shall exalt himself and magnify himself above every god. "The most high God" is the theme of the book of Daniel and the Antichrist is claiming to be better than the most high God. The phrase "he shall speak marvelous things against the God of gods" means he will blaspheme the one true God. In Revelation 13, another chapter dealing with the Antichrist, we read that he blasphemes Jesus Christ (Revelation 13:1, 5-6).

Daniel 11:37 says the Antichrist is going to rise above all gods, not just the one true God, but all false gods – exalting himself above them. It also says also he does not desire women. I believe that means the Antichrist will be a sodomite.

Daniel 11:38 talks about the Antichrist honoring the god of forces. This terminology means the Antichrist is going to be a military genius, one that will be able to lead the wars against Jesus Christ. The last war between Christ and Antichrist, when Jesus Christ returns to Jerusalem, will take place in the Jezreel Valley with the Antichrist as the leader alongside that which will energize him, Satan himself.

Antichrist is the first seal that will be released. A description of the Antichrist is found in Revelation 13. He's referred to as the "beast." Now that word is used a number of times in the book of Revelation, and it is always speaking about the Antichrist.

Revelation 13:1, *"And I stood upon the sand of the sea, and saw a beast rise up out of the sea, having seven heads and ten horns, and upon his horns ten crowns, and upon his heads the name of blasphemy."*

The False Church

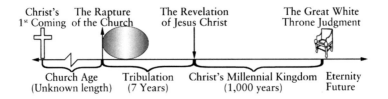

In Revelation 17, the word "beast" is used eight times in a description of the one who will lead the one-world false religion, ecclesiastical Babylon.

The word "whore" is used in this portion of Scripture three times while the word "woman" is used six times. A wicked woman is mentioned a total of nine times. Again, this is apocalyptic literature.

The Bible tells us that we are the bride of Christ; the true Church is the bride of Christ. A beautiful bride who comes down the church aisle, decked out in a beautiful, long, flowing white gown depicting the fact that she is pure as she comes to the altar to marry her partner for life. She is saying to the world, I am a virgin, I am a virtuous woman, and I come in purity to the time of my wedding.

The opposite of that would be a whore or a prostitute and that is what Revelation 17 is talking about. It speaks of a false church and that is what is going to be in place in the first 3½ years of the Tribulation Period.

As soon as the Antichrist is revealed, so also will this false church come into existence.

> Revelation 17:3, *"So he carried me away in the spirit into the wilderness: and I saw a woman sit upon a scarlet coloured beast, full of names of blasphemy, having seven heads and ten horns."*

Again, the theme of blasphemy is repeated. First in Daniel 11, again in Revelation 13, and lastly here again in Revelation 17. The Antichrist will blaspheme Jesus Christ and the false church will also be full of blasphemy.

Notice the 10 horns aspect of this beast. Here is another example of apocalyptic literature. This is the author using a symbol to communicate an absolute truth. Let us take a few moments to look at some of them. When we think about the 10 horns, we are thinking about the 10 horns of Daniel 7 and Revelation 13. Revelation 17 defines those 10 horns.

> Revelation 17:12-13, *"And the ten horns which thou sawest are ten kings, which have received no kingdom as yet; but receive power as kings one hour with the beast. These have one mind, and shall give their power and strength unto the beast."*

That is the Revived Roman Empire. This false church will also be a part of the Revived Roman Empire. Notice also that it has seven heads. The seven heads in Revelation 13:1 and 17:3 are defined in Revelation 17:9.

Revelation 17:9, *"And here is the mind which hath wisdom. The seven heads are seven mountains, on which the woman sitteth."*

The woman is the false church or whore. It will be headquartered in a seven-hilled city. I must remind you that in 95 A.D. when John the Apostle wrote the book of Revelation, the most important city – and especially the most important seven-hilled city in the entire world – was the city of Rome. So this false church will be headquartered in the city of Rome.

BABYLON, MOTHER OF HARLOTS

Revelation 17:5, *"And upon her forehead was a name written, MYSTERY, BABYLON THE GREAT, THE MOTHER OF HARLOTS AND ABOMINATIONS OF THE EARTH."*

The "mystery" part of "Mystery, Babylon" is not actually a part of the title, but just explaining that it is a mystery, so the title would be "Babylon the great, the Mother of Harlots and Abominations of the Earth." This is referring to the city of Babylon.

In Genesis 10, God tells Noah, Shem, Ham, and Japheth to be fruitful, multiply, and fill the earth. They endeavor to do just that. Ham has a son named Cush. Cush has a son named Nimrod. Genesis 10:10 says that Nimrod had a kingdom, and the beginning of his kingdom was Babel. Babel is the location known as Babylon today (which is still alive and well, by the way). We will get more in depth when we study Revelation 18 as we seek to learn about the truth of a literal Babylon.

> Genesis 11:4, *"And they said, Go to, let us build us a city and a tower, whose top may reach unto heaven; and let us make us a name, lest we be scattered abroad upon the face of the whole earth."*

What is being talked about here is the establishment of a false religion. The tower reaching into Heaven is a place of worship, and the "making of a name" is the naming of a false God. They weren't "making a name for themselves" as in becoming well known and popular. They were "making a name" to be worshipped, a false god. We are talking about everyone on earth being in one place; who was there to be impressed? They were building this city in direct opposition to the commandment of God. God told them to subdue the whole earth. They wanted to stay in one place.

Thus the Babylonian false religion began. Nimrod had a wife. Her name was Semiramis. Nimrod and Semiramis had a son. His name was Tammuz. They became the objects of worship. They were a mother-son cult. This was the Babylonian religion that was established by Nimrod there on the shores of the Euphrates River at Babylon. They did not like the name Jehovah God. They did not like to do what God said to do so they made themselves a name for a Babylonian god, Marduk.

Semiramis is referred to in the book of Jeremiah, not by her name but by her title in this mother-son cult. Jeremiah talks about Semiramis as the "queen of heaven" (Jeremiah 7:18, 44:17-25). She was worshipped on a special holy day called Ishtar. On this day they would paint these little boiled eggs with different colors and lay them out in the field and give the children a little basket to run out and pick up these colored eggs. Seem familiar? Those were the activities on this unholy day of worship of the queen of heaven, Ishtar.

Tammuz, the son of the mother-son cult is mentioned by the prophet Ezekiel. In Ezekiel 8, God brings Ezekiel back to the city of Jerusalem and walks him into the Temple. As they look around, there are all kinds of idolatrous portraits on the walls. He looks up and he sees a convent of virgins worshipping Tammuz (Ezekiel 8:14).

This mother-son cult was established at Babylon and would stay headquartered in Babylon until the fall of the Babylonian Empire in 539 B.C. At that time, this false Babylon religion moved its headquarters to the city of Pergamos (the third of the churches mentioned in Revelation 2). Pergamos is the location where they had started to deify the Roman emperors. The Roman Emperors had the political name of Caesar. Caesar is another word for emperor.

But they also had a name for their religious responsibilities. In Pergamos, I can show you the remains of statues that have engraved on the bottom the name for the religious responsibilities of these Caesars. That name was Pontifus Maximus. Pontifus Maximus means the major keeper of the bridge.

That was too long, so they shortened it to Pontiff, and then they had to shorten it later to Pope. They had priests who would serve them; they wore fish-shaped hats with scarlet and purple outfits. They had a convent of virgins.

Don't misunderstand what I am saying – I am talking about this mother-son cult, the Babylonian false religion headquartered at Pergamos. I am not talking about anything you may think I am talking about. I am simply talking about historic events that unfolded in the past.

> Revelation 17:16, *"And the ten horns which thou sawest upon the beast, these shall hate the whore, and shall make her desolate and naked, and shall eat her flesh, and burn her with fire."*

At the end of the first 3½ years of the Tribulation Period, the Revived Roman Empire is going to rise up and destroy the false church. The Revived Roman Empire (these 10 horns) is most likely the European Union of today. The potential similarities of these two entities only increased with the European Union's ratification of the Lisbon Treaty and the recent election of new leaders to take it into the future. That is another study for another time. But let me just simply say, if it is not the absolute fulfillment of the Revived Roman Empire,

75

the European Union of today is setting the infrastructure in place for Revelation 17 to be fulfilled.

Revelation 13 talks about the Antichrist who is the one who comes to power, the one who is energized by Satan.

> Revelation 13:2, *"And the beast which I saw was like unto a leopard, and his feet were as the feet of a bear, and his mouth as the mouth of a lion: and the dragon gave him his power, and his seat, and great authority."*

Revelation 12:9 describes the dragon as Satan himself.

> Revelation 13:11, *"And I beheld another beast coming up out of the earth; and he had two horns like a lamb, and he spake as a dragon."*

In verse 11 we see another beast. This one comes up out of the earth; this would be the False Prophet. So we have in place Satan, the one who energizes a human body to be Antichrist, and a False Prophet. The False Prophet, according to verses 12 and 13, will use signs, wonders, and miracles to deceive the entire world. All of this taking place as the Antichrist comes to power.

I happen to believe the Antichrist is alive and well on planet earth. I could have said that maybe 10 or 15 years ago, and it may or may not have been the same person. I believe Satan has an individual that he has selected standing by to be the one he will energize to raise to power as this world dictator, the Antichrist. Should that one die, or lose popularity, power, or position, Satan has another Antichrist candidate waiting in the wings. The Antichrist is the fulfillment of this first seal judgment, coming to establish a peace, establishing a false religion in the city of Rome, and putting events into motion that will begin the 7 years of terrible judgment upon the face of the earth. The Antichrist is the First Seal Judgment to be released by Jesus Christ according to Revelation 6:1-2.

The Two Witnesses

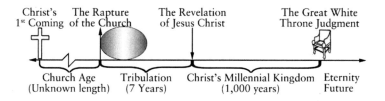

Christ's 1ˢᵗ Coming	The Rapture of the Church	The Revelation of Jesus Christ	The Great White Throne Judgment
Church Age (Unknown length)	Tribulation (7 Years)	Christ's Millennial Kingdom (1,000 years)	Eternity Future

The Time of Their Witness

In the first 3½ years of the Tribulation Period there is going to be a season of peace that coincides with the appearance of the Antichrist. Remember, the nations that will gather to attack the Jewish state of Israel will do so during a time when the Jews are dwelling safely in the land. This peace will come about because the Antichrist will confirm peace agreements between the Jewish people and their enemy neighbors (Daniel 9:27). The Antichrist will establish this peace; however, it is destined to be a short-term and false peace.

The clock starts ticking on the 7-year Tribulation when the Antichrist confirms the peace treaty. It is during that time that there will be two witnesses who will preach (Revelation 11).

> Revelation 11:3, *"And I will give power unto my two witnesses, and they shall prophesy a thousand two hundred and threescore days, clothed in sackcloth."*

That is 1,260 days; one-half of the 7-year period of time. Those are not Christian calendar days. Those would be Jewish calendar days. The Jewish calendar has only 360 days in it. The Jews have 12 months with 30 days each. They are on a lunar system and thus, 3½ years would be exactly 1,260 days.

The Christian calendar is solar, not lunar, so our 365-day years don't add up right with the timing laid out in Revelation. Taking 365 days times 7 years divided by 2 does not equal 1,260. But 360 days times 7 years divided by 2 does. This is another evidence that the focus is on the Jewish people during the 7-year Tribulation Period, not even a Christian calendar is being used to describe that time when the judgments will take place here on the earth.

God's Protection of the Two Witnesses

> Revelation 11:4-5, *"These are the two olive trees, and the two candlesticks standing before the God of the earth. And if any man will hurt them, fire proceedeth out of their mouth, and devoureth their enemies: and if any man will hurt them, he must in this manner be killed."*

That is amazing! The Two Witnesses will be protected for the first 3½ years of the Tribulation Period so that they may preach the gospel of the kingdom. Matthew 24:14 says that the gospel of the kingdom will be preached during the entire 7-years of the Tribulation. During the first half of the Tribulation period, 1260 days (Revelation 11:3), the Two Witnesses will preach the gospel of the kingdom. During the entire Tribulation the gospel of the kingdom will be preached by the 144,000 male virgin Jews. They will preach that the kingdom is coming and preach that the resurrected Jesus Christ is the one that they must trust in – His death, His burial, His resurrection – to be prepared for that kingdom.

These two witnesses will be protected while they are preaching and they will be headquartered on the Temple Mount in the city of Jerusalem. Not only will they be protected but also their power will be unbelievable.

> Revelation 11:6, *"These have power to shut heaven, that it rain not in the days of their prophecy: and have power over waters to turn them to blood, and to smite the earth with all plagues, as often as they will."*

If there is a purpose for presenting and displaying this power to the world, these two witnesses will have it available to do what God would have them to accomplish. They will reach the world with this gospel message. The preaching of the gospel of the kingdom which, at the end of the Tribulation, will culminate with the return of Jesus Christ.

> Revelation 11:7, *"And when they shall have finished their testimony, the beast that ascendeth out of the bottomless pit shall make war against them, and shall overcome them, and kill them."*

Notice what is going to happen next:

> Revelation 11:8-9, *"And their dead bodies shall lie in the street of the great city, which spiritually is called Sodom and Egypt, where also our Lord was crucified. And they of the people and kindreds and tongues and nations shall see their dead bodies three days and an half, and shall not suffer their dead bodies to be put in graves."*

The "great city" is the city of Jerusalem. And so, after 3½ years of ministry, these two witnesses are killed and their bodies will be left in the streets. They will lay there and everybody on earth will see them.

> Revelation 11:10, *"And their dead bodies shall lie in the street of the great city, which spiritually is called Sodom and Egypt, where also our Lord was crucified. And they of the people and kindreds and tongues and nations shall see their dead bodies three days and an half, and shall not suffer their dead bodies to be put in graves. And they that dwell upon the earth shall rejoice over them, and make merry, and shall send gifts one to another; because these two prophets tormented them that dwelt on the earth."*

During this time, there is going to be partying going on across the world. It's going to be a dead party and they are going to exchange gifts with one another. The world will rejoice following the death of these two witnesses. However, their rejoicing is abruptly and amazingly cut short after just a few days.

> Revelation 11:11-12, *"And after three days and an half the Spirit of life from God entered into them, and they stood upon their feet; and great fear fell upon them which saw them. And they heard a great voice from heaven saying unto them, Come up hither. And they ascended up to heaven in a cloud; and their enemies beheld them."*

Did you notice that phrase again? "Come up hither." Remember, that is what was said in Revelation 4:1 to John, at the Rapture of the Church. Now, in similar fashion, the two witnesses ascended into Heaven in a cloud and their enemies beheld them. That ends the ministry of the two witnesses at the conclusion of the first 3½ years of the Tribulation Period.

The Identities of the Witnesses

There is much speculation as to the identities of the two witnesses. I have an idea who I believe they are. We will look at that in just a moment, but let me show you a very interesting idea that you may have never considered before. The fact is that these two witnesses, as with any witness, give testimony of what they have seen. Let's explore that a moment.

Luke 24 is dealing with the time of the resurrection of Jesus Christ. The first verse is talking about how on the first day of the week when Mary the mother of Jesus, Mary Magdalene, and the Mary of "Mary and Martha," come to the location where Jesus Christ had been buried for the purpose of anointing his body with spices.

> Luke 24:2-4, *"And they found the stone rolled away from the sepulchre. And they entered in, and found not the body of the Lord Jesus. And it came to pass, as they were much perplexed thereabout, behold, two men stood by them in shining garments."*

Isn't that interesting? Two men stood there by the graveside and there was no Jesus Christ in that grave. The stone had been rolled away and the grave was open; it's unbelievable what had happened, and these two men witnessed what took place. They had witnessed the resurrection of Jesus Christ.

Now let me show you something else that continues along this line. Acts 1 is the record of that 40-day period after the resurrection of Jesus Christ when He taught His disciples about things to come (prophecy). This teaching was preparing the minds of the disciples to eventually reach the entire world with the gospel message.

He concludes that teaching by telling them to wait there in Jerusalem for the power that is going to make them witnesses unto the entire world starting in Jerusalem, going to Judea, and Samaria, and unto the uttermost parts of the earth.

> Acts 1:10-11, *"And while they looked stedfastly toward heaven as he went up, behold, two men stood by them in white apparel; Which also said, Ye men of Galilee, why stand ye gazing up into heaven? this same Jesus, which is taken up from you into heaven, shall so come in like manner as ye have seen him go into heaven."*

Here we see two men witnessing the ascension of Christ into Heaven. They said that He is coming back the same way. Might I suggest to you that these are the two witnesses of Revelation 11. Two men who saw the resurrection of Jesus Christ and could give testimony that He was alive as He said He would be. And because He had resurrected from the dead, He was who He said He was and could do what He said He would do, give eternal life to all of those who come unto Him.

These two witnessed the ascension of Christ and they gave testimony that as He had gone away, so He should come again one day. There were two witnesses of the resurrection and the ascension of Christ into Heaven. That will be the message that they will be preaching during this time (the first half of the Tribulation Period).

Now, let me tell you what I believe is the identity of these two witnesses. The Bible clearly talks about the identity of one of them and even gives his name. This witness is talked about in the next-to-last verse, in the last chapter, of the last book of the Old Testament (Malachi 4:5). These will be the last words that God gives to humankind before a 400-year period, mostly silent, before sending the incarnate Word, Jesus Christ, and then beginning the New Testament.

> Malachi 4:5, *"Behold, I will send you Elijah the prophet before the coming of the great and dreadful day of the LORD."*

You know, John the Baptist could have been the one who fulfilled this promise. In Matthew 11:10-15, Jesus says that John was indeed capable of fulfilling the promise, but the Jewish people rejected him, thus an Elijah must come. So one of these two witnesses has to be Elijah.

Genesis 5 reveals who I believe the second of the two witnesses will be. Genesis 5 is a genealogy. You know, you can learn a lot from studying genealogies.

> Genesis 5:22-24, *"And Enoch walked with God after he begat Methuselah three hundred years, and begat sons and daughters: And all the days of Enoch were three hundred sixty and fi ve years: And Enoch walked with God: and he was not; for God took him."*

I would suggest that the two witnesses will be Elijah and Enoch. Why these two?. Because these two men have never died. The Bible says in Hebrews 9:27, "And as it is appointed unto men once to die, but after this the judgment." Elijah, a godly prophet, never experienced physical death, but was taken into Heaven by a

84

whirlwind. Enoch, too, walked with God. He walked with God on the earth, and then he walked right into Heaven.

These two men will come back, one a Gentile, one a Jew, reaching out to the Gentiles and the Jews who will remain on the earth with the gospel message: Jesus Christ died, was buried, resurrected, ascended into Heaven, and is coming again. The two witnesses will be in ministry during the first 3½ years of the Tribulation.

The 144,000

A product of the witnessing and preaching of these two witnesses will be the salvation, the evangelization of 144,000 male, virgin Jews. Revelation 7 gives us the number and it gives us the tribes from which they come

> Revelation 7:4, *"And I heard the number of them which were sealed:* and there were *sealed an hundred* and *forty* and *four thousand of all the tribes of the children of Israel."*

The Bible says earlier in Revelation 7 that God will seal these men so that they can spread the gospel across the entire world during this Tribulation. The judgments, according to Revelation 7:3, cannot even begin until these servants are sealed.

I call the 144,000 "male virgin Jews" because of a parallel passage in Revelation 14. Revelation 14:4 gives us the details on these 144,000. As we jump around in the book of Revelation, remember that it does not unfold numerically, but instead chronologically.

Revelation 14:1, 4, *"And I looked, and, lo, a Lamb stood on the mount Sion, and with him an hundred forty and four thousand, having his Father's name written in their foreheads.... These are they which were not defiled with women; for they are virgins. These are they which follow the Lamb whithersoever he goeth. These were redeemed from among men, being the firstfruits unto God and to the Lamb."*

Mount Sion, or Zion, is the city of Jerusalem. There will be 144,000 male virgin Jews who will travel across the world preaching the gospel. They will be those who are going to be in ministry, preaching the gospel – the death, the burial, the resurrection of Christ – and the coming kingdom that Jesus Christ will set up. That's the message they will be preaching. That is the gospel of the kingdom. Matthew 24:14 says that each and every person on earth is going to hear this message before Jesus Christ comes back and will have an opportunity to receive Jesus Christ as their Lord and Savior.

The Hopeless Lost

There is one exception. 2 Thessalonians 2:8-12 says anyone left after the Rapture of the Church that has heard, understood, and rejected the gospel will be sent a strong delusion by God. He will blind them so that they believe the lie of Satan and they will accept the Antichrist. That is the reason that Jewish people will accept a Gentile, the Antichrist, to be their true Messiah. How could a Gentile be the Jewish Messiah? He cannot, but because God will cause those that have rejected Jesus Christ as Lord and Savior to believe the lie of Satan, they will accept this Gentile, the Antichrist, as their messiah.

These 144,000 male virgin Jews will go preaching the gospel in the region. Since they are virgins, they do not have a family to take their focus away from what God has called them to do. They only have 7 years to get this gospel message out to the entire world. The two witnesses preach, 144,000 male virgin Jews get saved, they go across the world preaching the gospel, and it is during that time that many who had not heard the gospel before the Rapture will come to know Jesus Christ as Lord and Savior.

> Revelation 7:9, *"After this I beheld, and, lo, a great multitude, which no man could number, of all nations, and kindreds, and people, and tongues, stood before the throne, and before the Lamb, clothed with white robes, and palms in their hands."*

The Seal Judgments Continued

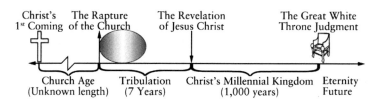

Christ's   The Rapture   The Revelation   The Great White
1ˢᵗ Coming of the Church   of Jesus Christ   Throne Judgment

Church Age   Tribulation   Christ's Millennial Kingdom   Eternity
(Unknown length)   (7 Years)   (1,000 years)   Future

The Second Seal Judgment, Revelation 6:3-4, *"And when he had opened the second seal, I heard the second beast say, Come and see. And there went out another horse that was red: and power was given to him that sat thereon to take peace from the earth, and that they should kill one another: and there was given unto him a great sword."*

This man on the red horse, the second seal judgment, will be the judgment of war. There is going to be an alignment of nations that will come against the Jewish state early on in the Tribulation Period. Daniel 11:40-44 gives us some of those nations. It talks about the king of the North, Syria, and the king of the South, Egypt, joining forces with additional nations that come to try to destroy the Jewish state. Ezekiel 38:2-6 lists Magog (Gog is the person, the leader of the place, which is Magog), Persia, Ethiopia, Libya, Meshech, Tubal, Gomer, and Togarmah.

Let me give you the hermeneutical principle. (Hermeneutics means interpretive or explanatory Bible study.) This principle relates to Biblical geography. When trying to figure out where a given place is, ask yourself who was the author writing about when he wrote the book? In this case, who was Ezekiel writing about when he wrote his prophecy some 2,500 years ago? What was Magog at that time? You can look at an ancient Biblical map and determine that Magog was that piece of real estate north of the Caspian and Black Seas, which would be modern-day Russia.

88

Following this principle, I will tell you the modern-day nations spoken of in Ezekiel 38. Magog is Russia and the Ukraine. Meshech, Tubal, Gomer, and Togarmah is modern-day Turkey. Until 1936, Afghanistan, Pakistan, and Iran were known as Persia. Ethiopia, or Cush as it is known in some Bible translations, is Ethiopia, Somalia, and Sudan. Then it mentions Libya, or Put, the modern Libya. In Psalm 83 it also mentions the Ishmaelites (v.6), that would be Saudi Arabia, and Tyre (v.7) is Lebanon.

These nations: Syria, Egypt, Russia, Iran, Afghanistan, Pakistan, Turkey, Ethiopia, Somalia, Sudan, Libya, Saudi Arabia, and Lebanon will form a coalition and come against Israel in the Tribulation. Those are the major players that you read about and this will be the next judgment after the appearance of the Antichrist – War, the man on the red horse (Revelation 6).

> The Third Seal Judgment, Revelation 6:5-6, *"And when he had opened the third seal, I heard the third beast say, Come and see. And I beheld, and lo a black horse; and he that sat on him had a pair of balances in his hand. And I heard a voice in the midst of the four beasts say, A measure of wheat for a penny, and three measures of barley for a penny; and see thou hurt not the oil and the wine."*

Here we see the third seal and the third horseman, famine. People all over the world will be going daily without food, and many will starve to death. To get enough wheat to make bread for a family of four for one day, you would have to pay a "penny." A "penny" or "denarius" in Roman times was commonly thought of as a day's wages. Three measures of barley are enough to feed your animals that day. Famine will run rampant. When millions lay down their plows to pick up their swords to fight in the wars from the second seal judgment, then the farmers do not produce and famine will soon follow.

> The Fourth Seal Judgment, Revelation 6:7-8, "*And when he had opened the fourth seal, I heard the voice of the fourth beast say, Come and see. And I looked, and behold a pale horse: and his name that sat on him was Death, and Hell followed with him. And power was given unto them over the fourth part of the earth, to kill with sword, and with hunger, and with death, and with the beasts of the earth.*"

One-fourth of the entire population of this earth will be killed when the fourth seal judgment is released. One out of every four persons on the earth will die at this time. At our present population of 6.8 billion people on the earth, that would be 1.7 billion people who will die when this judgment is released.

Chart: The Four Horsemen of Revelation

Horse Color	Rider / Judgment
White	Antichrist
Red	War
Black	Famine
Pale	Death

The Fifth Seal Judgment, Revelation 6:9-11, *"And when he had opened the fifth seal, I saw under the altar the souls of them that were slain for the word of God, and for the testimony which they held: And they cried with a loud voice, saying, How long, O Lord, holy and true, dost thou not judge and avenge our blood on them that dwell on the earth? And white robes were given unto every one of them; and it was said unto them, that they should rest yet for a little season, until their fellowservants also and their brethren, that should be killed as they were, should be fulfilled."*

During this Tribulation Period, through the ministry of the two witnesses and the 144,000, there will be a large number of people who will turn to Christ (Revelation 7:9). Please note, these will not be Christians. Remember, there are three strands to the human family, and the Christians have been Raptured out of the world before the Tribulation. These Tribulation saints will either be Jews or Gentiles – not Christians – but Jews or Gentiles who believe. The passage in Revelation 6 indicates that many of these believing Jews and believing Gentiles become martyrs for the testimony that they have of Jesus Christ. That is the fifth seal judgment, the martyrdom of the Tribulation saints.

The Sixth Seal Judgment, Revelation 6:12-14, *"And I beheld when he had opened the sixth seal, and, lo, there was a great earthquake; and the sun became black as sackcloth of hair, and the moon became as blood; And the stars of*

92

heaven fell unto the earth, even as a fig tree cas-
teth her untimely figs, when she is shaken of a
mighty wind. And the heaven departed as a
scroll when it is rolled together; and every
mountain and island were moved out of their
places."

The sixth seal is signs in the heavens. The sun starts to go out, the moon starts to turn to the color of blood. Remember the moon reflects the sun's light and when the sun loses its light, what happens? Have you ever seen at the time of sunset how, when the moon has popped up and it looks almost red in color, and the clouds around it look the same, it's an amazing and beautiful scene to see. But when the sun goes dark and the moon turns blood red in the sky, it will not be beautiful, it will be terrifying.

These events share a very interesting connection to the Olivet Discourse of Matthew 24. Jesus told His disciples that there would be many deceivers claiming to be the Christ, like the Antichrist (v.4-5, 11, 24) of the first seal. He then warned of wars and rumors of wars (v.6-7a), the second seal; then famines, the third seal; and pestilences, which leads to death (v.7b), the fourth seal. He even warns of His followers being killed for their faith (v.9), which is the fifth seal. He talks about earthquakes in diverse places, that happens here in the sixth seal judgment. Remember, no prophecy is of private interpretation, and to understand

Scripture, you have to compare Scripture with other passages of Scripture.

> Matthew 24:32-34, "*Now learn a parable of the fig tree; When his branch is yet tender, and putteth forth leaves, ye know that summer is nigh: So likewise ye, when ye shall see all these things, know that it is near, even at the doors. Verily I say unto you, This generation shall not pass, till all these things be fulfilled.*"

Jesus says that we must understand prophecy so that we might be able to look at what is going on, compare it to Scripture, and know where we are in God's prophetic plan.

The Seventh Seal

> Revelation 8:1, "*And when he had opened the seventh seal, there was silence in heaven about the space of half an hour.*"

I believe the Bible teaches in Hebrews 12 that the people in Heaven are able to see the events taking place on the earth. So as the events of the Tribulation unfold, those of us in Heaven will be aware of the suffering below. Many will have friends and family that will be going through this terrible time of judgment. I believe this half hour of silence is a time of mourning for the suffering that is taking place.

God does not enjoy punishing the wicked (Ezekiel 18:23, 32, 33:11; 2 Peter 3:9). He wants everyone to repent, be saved, and live. When we are in Heaven, we will be like Him. We will be separated from sin and

94

share a sinless nature with God. So we, too, will take no pleasure in the death of the wicked. We will grieve over the suffering. The suffering is deserved, it is just, and holiness demands that sin be punished, but it is not something God enjoys having to do. So for this half hour of silence, I believe, we will be acknowledging and mourning what is taking place on earth.

We will grieve, but I do not believe that we will be so burdened with what we see that we will not be able to stand it while we are in Heaven. The Bible doesn't say that the tears are going to be wiped away at the Rapture of the Church, or the battle of Armageddon, or during the Millennial Kingdom, or even at the Great White Throne Judgment. It's in the time of Eternity Future with the New Heavens and the New Earth and the New Jerusalem that all tears are wiped away (Revelation 21:4). So there will be some sorrow, even in Heaven, but it will be a controllable sorrow, as we look upon all of these people who have meant so much to us going through this judgment.

These are the Seven Seal Judgments. There yet remain the trumpet judgments (Revelation 8), and the Seven Vial Judgments (Revelation 16).

Chart: The Seven Seal Judgments

	Seal	Details
1	Rider on a White Horse - Antichrist	The false messiah takes control of this world – politically, militarily, economically, and religiously.
2	Rider on a Red Horse - War	Nations align against Israel: Syria, Egypt, Iran, Russia, Afghanistan, Sudan, Pakistan, Ethiopia, Somalia, Libya, Turkey, Saudi Arabia, Lebanon (Daniel 11:40-45; Ezekiel 38:2, 5; Psalm 83).
3	Rider on a Black Horse - Famine	Farmers use their time and resources for war – food becomes scarce. Starvation kills millions.
4	Rider on a Pale Horse - Death	Death and Hell come to earth. One fourth of the world's human population is taken to the grave.
5	Martyrdom	Many who come to Christ through the two witnesses and the 144,000 will be murdered for their faith.
6	Signs in the heavens, earthquakes	The sun becomes black. The moon becomes as blood. Stars fall to earth. Every mountain and island is moved.
7	Silence, Trumpets	Silence in Heaven for about a half hour. Trumpet Judgments begin.

Revelation: A Chronology   Dr. Jimmy DeYoung

THE MIDPOINT OF THE TRIBULATION

The Angelic Wars

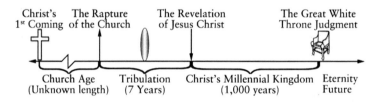

The Seven Seal Judgments will take place at the same time as the ministry of the two witnesses and the 144,000 male virgin Jews. All of these events take place in the first 3½ years of the Tribulation. At the end of those first 3½ years, there will be an event that will take place in Heaven and ultimately end up on the earth.

Revelation 12:7-9, *"And there was war in heaven: Michael and his angels fought against the dragon; and the dragon fought and his angels, And prevailed not; neither was their place found any more in heaven. And the great dragon was cast out, that old serpent, called the Devil, and Satan, which deceiveth the whole world: he was cast out into the earth, and his angels were cast out with him."*

At this point, the Devil and the angels who have been following him instead of God will no longer have access to Heaven. They are being kicked out.

Remember, there are three heavens. Paul wrote about a man going to the "third heaven" in 2 Corinthians 12. I believe Paul was talking about himself, but that is another discussion. Since there is a third heaven, there must be a first and a second heaven. The first heaven is the sky, sometimes in the Bible called "the firmament." The second heaven is outer space, the area where the stars are. The third, of course, where Jesus Christ sits to the right hand side of God the Father, and where we Christians will be during the Tribulation. So we see the first heaven by day, the second heaven by night, and the third heaven by faith.

Angels in Prophecy

"Angel," or the plural form "angels," is the most used noun in the book of Revelation. It is used 81 times and refers to both good angels and evil angels. Let's take a moment to see where angels came from, and the role they have played in the past, and will play according to Bible prophecy in the future.

> Colossians 1:16, *"For by him were all things created, that are in heaven, and that are in earth, visible and invisible, whether* they be *thrones, or dominions, or principalities, or powers: all things were created by him, and for him."*

Jesus Christ created everything. So it is Jesus Christ that is the Creator being spoken of in the Law of the Sabbath, the fourth of the Ten Commandments.

> Exodus 20:11, *"For in six days the LORD made heaven and earth, the sea, and all that in them is, and rested the seventh day: wherefore the LORD blessed the sabbath day, and hallowed it."*

You can study Genesis 1, which is the record of the six days of creation, and you will not find a statement that says, "On the ___ day, God said let there be angels, and there were angels." But He did create them. So to figure out when, you have to do a little digging through God's Word, compare Scripture to Scripture and come to a conclusion.

> Job 38:4-7, *"Where wast thou when I laid the foundations of the earth? declare, if thou hast understanding. Who hath laid the measures thereof, if thou knowest? or who hath stretched the line upon it? Whereupon are the foundations thereof fastened? or who laid the corner stone*

*thereof; When the morning stars sang together,
and all the sons of God shouted for joy?"*

God is speaking to Job, asking by what right does he question the choices that God has made, since he wasn't there when God created the Universe and cannot even explain how it works, much less improve upon it. Compare verses 4 and 7, and notice the word "when." When God laid the foundations of the earth, and when the morning stars sang and all the sons of God shouted. The phrases "morning stars" and "sons of God" both refer to angels. What God is saying is that when He created the world, the angels were there, and they welcomed what God had just accomplished in bringing the earth into existence.

Therefore, angels must have been created on the first day (Genesis 1:1), after God had created the heavens (the heavens had to be first so that the angels could have somewhere to exist), and before He created the earth (so that they would be able to rejoice at its creation). All the angels were there on the first day, and they were all good angels at that time.

Genesis 1:31, *"And God saw every thing that he had made, and, behold, it was very good. And the evening and the morning were the sixth day."*

I love what the Hebrew says there. Not only very good, but abundantly excellent. There were no evil angels at this point. Satan was not "Satan" the enemy on this sixth day of creation. God did not create evil an-

102

gels. God created good angels, some of which decided to become evil – just as Adam and Eve were created sinless and chose to become sinful.

The angel that would later become Satan did exist on the sixth day of creation, but as Lucifer, the most prominent of all the cherubs placed over the throne of God and all of creation (Isaiah 14, Ezekiel 28). He rebelled against God sometime between the events of Genesis 1:31 and Genesis 3:1 when he appears as the deceiver, that old serpent, the Devil.

At the midway point of the Tribulation, Satan is going to lead an army of evil angels, one-third of all the angels ever created, against God. These evil angels are going to be defeated and thrown out of the heavens by Michael, the commander in chief of the good angels in Heaven.

After they are cast out of Heaven, they are going to persecute the Jewish people during that last 3½ years of the Tribulation. They will attack with all the force they can to destroy the Jewish people. Verses 13 and 17 in Revelation 12 talk about Satan knowing he only has a little time available and he will use what time he has to try to wipe out the Jewish people. If Satan can destroy the Jewish people, then God's plan fails and he is not able to keep his promise to the Jewish people. But rest assured, God will keep all of His promises, and that includes Satan's ultimate defeat.

Revelation 12:7-8, *"And there was war in heaven: Michael and his angels fought against*

103

the dragon; and the dragon fought and his angels, And prevailed not; neither was their place found any more in heaven."

These evil angels are not going to be thrown out of the third heaven, because they are not in the third heaven. Only one evil angel, according to Revelation 12:10, has access to the throne of God to accuse the brethren on a daily basis. That is Satan himself.

In Lucifer's rebellion, he became Satan and convinced one-third of the angels to rebel against God with him. Those rebellious angels were cast out of the third heaven into the first or the second heaven. Here is why I say that:

Ephesians 6:12, *"For we wrestle not against flesh and blood, but against principalities, against powers, against the rulers of the darkness of this world, against spiritual wickedness in high places."*

That is talking about the fallen angels in high places, like the first and second heaven. Ephesians 2:2 calls Satan the "prince of the power of the air"; that's the first heaven. At the angelic rebellion, Satan was cast to the first heaven. That's right, above us, where the sun and the clouds are located; or even into the second heaven, where the stars are located. In that particular location, Satan and his evil angels are headquartered now, with Satan dispatching evil angels to the earth.

The Trumpet Judgments

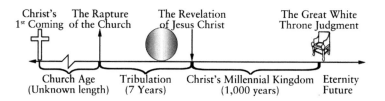

In Revelation 6 it talked about the Lamb, Jesus Christ, opening each of the sealed judgments. However, Jesus uses angels to sound the Seven Trumpets Judgment and then to pour out the Seven Vial Judgments.

The First Trumpet Judgment, Revelation 8:7, *"The first angel sounded, and there followed hail and fire mingled with blood, and they were cast upon the earth: and the third part of trees was burnt up, and all green grass was burnt up."*

This passage is describing ecological judgment upon all the earth. Believe what you will about global warming or climate change, but there is going to be supernatural ecological judgment during the coming Tribulation Period.

The Second Trumpet Judgment, Revelation 8:8-9, *"And the second angel sounded, and as it were a great mountain burning with fire was cast into the sea: and the third part of the sea became blood; And the third part of the creatures which were in the sea, and had life, died; and the third part of the ships were destroyed."*

105

The Third Trumpet Judgment, Revelation 8:10-11, *"And the third angel sounded, and there fell a great star from heaven, burning as it were a lamp, and it fell upon the third part of the rivers, and upon the fountains of waters; And the name of the star is called Wormwood: and the third part of the waters became wormwood; and many men died of the waters, because they were made bitter."*

The waters, the fresh waters, the rivers, the ponds, and the lakes upon the earth will become bitter and many people who drink from these fountains of water shall die. Having fresh, clean, drinkable water is vital to sustaining human life. This judgment will take that away.

The Fourth Trumpet Judgment, Revelation 8:12, *"And the fourth angel sounded, and the third part of the sun was smitten, and the third part of the moon, and the third part of the stars; so as the third part of them was darkened, and the day shone not for a third part of it, and the night likewise."*

Another sign in Heaven, that is the fourth trumpet judgment.

The Fifth Trumpet Judgment, Revelation 9:1, *"And the fifth angel sounded, and I saw a star fall from heaven unto the earth: and to him was given the key of the bottomless pit."*

This is not a star like the stars in the night sky. Remember, the word "star" can refer to angels. We see here that the "star" is given the key to unlock the Bottomless Pit.

The Bottomless Pit

> Revelation 9:2, *"And he opened the bottomless pit; and there arose a smoke out of the pit, as the smoke of a great furnace; and the sun and the air were darkened by reason of the smoke of the pit. And there came out of the smoke locusts upon the earth: and unto them was given power, as the scorpions of the earth have power."*

Who are these that will be in the Bottomless Pit? They will be evil angels released from the Bottomless Pit that will come upon the earth and join the other evil angels under the leadership of Satan as they attempt to destroy the Jewish people.

Genesis 6 explains that there was fornication between angels and human women. That was the reason for the Flood. The terms used are "the sons of God" and "the daughters of men." As we saw earlier in Job, and throughout the Old Testament, angels are referred to as "the sons of God." These fallen angels and human women came together physically and produced children. The angel-human hybrids came into existence with a bloodline that is Satanic in its origins.

> Genesis 3:15, *"And I will put enmity between thee and the woman, and between thy seed and her seed; it shall bruise thy head, and thou shalt bruise his heel."*

107

This is the first promise of a Messiah, sometimes this verse is called the "Proto-Evangelium" or first gospel. It was actually spoken by God to the serpent. Satan knew from then on that God had a plan to destroy him through the Messiah. Satan's main purpose therefore became preventing the Messiah from coming. Through this ungodly coupling between fallen angels and humans, Satan was attempting to contaminate the human bloodline. Jude 6 and 7 talks about angels who have committed fornication. This is the only time in history when that could have happened.

Some might argue that angels are not married or given in marriage. The Bible doesn't say that. What Jesus does say is that the angels "in Heaven" are neither married nor given in marriage (Matthew 22:30, Mark 12:25). This does not mean that angels are incapable of having a sexual relationship on earth, just that they do not do so in Heaven – just as we will not engage in those activities in Heaven.

The Bible tells us that angels can take on the forms of human beings. In Genesis 19, Lot saw two angels walk into Sodom, invited them to come to his house, and prepared a meal for them. They had a capability of eating a meal. He washed their feet. They were in the form of men. Now either they were in the form of men, or they were a couple of feet, a hand, and a mouth floating around.

Suffice it to say, there were evil angels that had children with human women, and the purpose for the

Flood was to wipe out that satanic bloodline in humankind. These angels that committed that dastardly act some 4,500 years ago are held in the Bottomless Pit until they are released in the fifth trumpet judgment.

When they are released from that Bottomless Pit, they will take on the form of locusts. Not locusts like you have ever recognized, they will be nothing like grasshoppers.

> Revelation 9:7-10, *"And the shapes of the locusts were like unto horses prepared unto battle; and on their heads were as it were crowns like gold, and their faces were as the faces of men. And they had hair as the hair of women, and their teeth were as the teeth of lions. And they had breastplates, as it were breastplates of iron; and the sound of their wings was as the sound of chariots of many horses running to battle. And they had tails like unto scorpions, and there were stings in their tails: and their power was to hurt men five months."*

These are alien creatures invading the earth. They are locust-shaped animals or creatures, and they are not like any other grasshopper you have ever seen. They have the face of a man, the teeth of a lion and the hair of a woman. They have a breastplate. They have scorpion's tails, and they can torment men for five months. These invaders come to the earth and join with Satan and all the evil angels to try to destroy the Jewish people so that God's plan cannot be fulfilled. These are UFOs – unidentified flying objects. Now I do not be-

109

lieve that there is any life on any other planet in the universe, but I do believe that Satan and his evil angels are in the first heaven right above us. And Satan can dispatch these evil angels to the earth, therefore making them alien, foreign, and from the second heaven, which is outer space.

The Sixth and Seventh Trumpet Judgments

> The Sixth Trumpet Judgment, Revelation 9:13-16, *"And the sixth angel sounded, and I heard a voice from the four horns of the golden altar which is before God, Saying to the sixth angel which had the trumpet, Loose the four angels which are bound in the great river Euphrates. And the four angels were loosed, which were prepared for an hour, and a day, and a month, and a year, for to slay the third part of men. And the number of the army of the horsemen were two hundred thousand thousand: and I heard the number of them."*

That is 200 million evil angels killing 1 out of every 3 human beings upon the face of the earth. Remember the fourth seal judgment, (Revelation 6:7-8), one-fourth of the human population has already been wiped out, and now we have one-third of those that remain. That means half of the total human population that entered into the Tribulation are now dead. Using today's population of 6.8 billion people, that would mean 3.4 billion men, women, and children would have died since the beginning of the Tribulation, and it's barely half over.

110

The Seventh Trumpet Judgment, Revelation 11:15, *"And the seventh angel sounded; and there were great voices in heaven, saying, The kingdoms of this world are become the kingdoms of our Lord, and of his Christ; and he shall reign for ever and ever."*

This is a glimpse of what is going to happen in the future. This is not talking about the event happening at this point because out of this seventh trumpet judgment comes the Seven Vial Judgments of Revelation 16. Now these judgments of chapter 16 are going to unfold very quickly, but it is not the end. The kingdom is not yet being set up. It is just a vision of what is going to happen in the future.

Chart: The Seven Trumpet Judgments

	Trumpets	Details
1	One-third of the Earth burned	Hail, fire mingled with blood burns one-third of all the trees and grass.
2	One-third of all sea creatures die	One-third of the sea becomes blood. One-third of the creatures that were in the sea die. One-third of the ships are destroyed.
3	Stars fall; one-third of water turns bitter	One-third of the rivers and fountains of waters become wormwood (bitter, poison) and many die.
4	One-third sun, moon, and stars darkened	One-third of the sun is smitten, one-third of the moon and one-third of the stars are darkened.
5	Woes, Abaddon, Locusts	Woes pronounced against man. Fallen angels, like locust, are released from the bottomless pit to torment men for months, under their king, Abaddon or Apollyon (Satan).
6	One-third of people killed by horsemen	200 million evil angels as horsemen will kill one-third of humans. Half the world – 3 billion people – is dead by the midpoint of the Tribulation.
7	Wrath / Reward	A vision of the future yet to come. *"The kingdoms of this world are becoming the kingdoms of our Lord, and of His Christ; and He shall reign forever and ever."*

The Vial Judgments

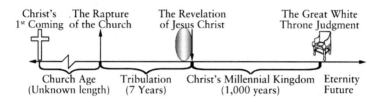

Christ's   The Rapture   The Revelation   The Great White
1ˢᵗ Coming of the Church   of Jesus Christ   Throne Judgment

Church Age   Tribulation   Christ's Millennial Kingdom   Eternity
(Unknown length)   (7 Years)   (1,000 years)   Future

Revelation 16:1, *"And I heard a great voice out of the temple saying to the seven angels, Go your ways, and pour out the vials of the wrath of God upon the earth."*

Here we have the beginning of the Seven Vial Judgments. That's vial like a pitcher, pot, or bowl; not vile like evil, wicked, or bad. These seven judgments will literally be poured out upon the earth, like water from a pitcher.

The First Vial Judgment, Revelation 16:2, *"And the first went, and poured out his vial upon the earth; and there fell a noisome and grievous sore upon the men which had the mark of the beast, and* upon *them which worshipped his image."*

Those who reject Jesus Christ will take the "mark of the beast" (some type of identification mark) on their forehead or on their right hand. Well, they are going to have grievous sores come upon them when this first vial is released.

The Second Vial Judgment, Revelation 16:3, *"And the second angel poured out his vial upon*

113

the sea; and it became as the blood of a dead
man: *and every living soul died in the sea."*

Remember, it was one-third of those living souls in
the sea that were destroyed in the second trumpet
judgment. At the second vial, every living creature left
in the sea will die.

The Third Vial Judgment, Revelation 16:4-7,
*"And the third angel poured out his vial upon
the rivers and fountains of waters; and they became blood. And I heard the angel of the waters
say, Thou art righteous, O Lord, which art, and
wast, and shalt be, because thou hast judged
thus. For they have shed the blood of saints and
prophets, and thou hast given them blood to
drink; for they are worthy. And I heard another
out of the altar say, Even so, Lord God Almighty, true and righteous* are *thy judgments."*

The third trumpet judgment that just turned the
water bitter is now going to be overshadowed by the
third vial judgment that turns all the water on the earth
to blood.

The Fourth Vial Judgment, Revelation 16:8-9,
*"And the fourth angel poured out his vial upon
the sun; and power was given unto him to
scorch men with fi re. And men were scorched
with great heat, and blasphemed the name of
God, which hath power over these plagues: and
they repented not to give him glory."*

The fourth vial is related to the fourth trumpet
judgment. Where once the sun became dark, now it

burns hotter than ever. Notice that, even in judgment, the man who has turned against God will not repent.

> The Fifth Vial Judgment, Revelation 16:10-11, *"And the fifth angel poured out his vial upon the seat of the beast; and his kingdom was full of darkness; and they gnawed their tongues for pain, And blasphemed the God of heaven because of their pains and their sores, and repented not of their deeds."*

The pain of the fifth vial judgment is so intense that men will chew on their tongues to try to relieve the pain. Once again, judgment that is designed to convict men of their sin is met with further rebellion, and even blasphemy.

> The Sixth Vial Judgment, Revelation 16:12, *"And the sixth angel poured out his vial upon the great river Euphrates; and the water thereof was dried up, that the way of the kings of the east might be prepared."*

In the Bible, all directions are from the starting point of Jerusalem (Ezekiel 5:5). So the "kings of the east" are east of Jerusalem. That includes the nations of China and India. Those two nations alone make up more than one-third of the earth's total population. Today, China has about 1.33 billion people and India about 1.17 billion. That is 2.5 billion people, close to 37 percent of the world's 6.8 billion.

The river Euphrates is a natural border between the Middle East and the Far East. It will be dried up to make way for the kings of the East to enter into Jerusalem. Zechariah 14 talks about all the nations of the world gathering at Jerusalem. That is the beginning of the campaign of Armageddon. This is going to be a campaign, not merely a single battle. It will indeed be the mother of all battles, and it will take place beginning in Jerusalem, culminating in the Jezreel Valley in the center part of the state of Israel. The kings of the East will have made their way made to Jerusalem thanks to the Euphrates being dried up in the sixth vial judgment. They will join with Satan as they take on the returning Messiah, Jesus Christ, who comes back to the Mount of Olives in the city of Jerusalem.

Notice the parenthetical passage found in Revelation 16:13-16. It lists the Satanic Trinity (Satan, Antichrist, and the False Prophet) using signs, wonders, and miracles to gather all the nations of the world into Jerusalem. This is the beginning of the Campaign of Armageddon.

Chart: The Seven Vial Judgments

	Vials	Details
1	Plague of terrible sores	Grievous sores come upon everyone who has denied Jesus Christ, who did not receive Him, who rejected Him so that they received the mark of the beast, 666, and believed the lie of the Antichrist.
2	Sea turns to blood, All sea life dies	All of the seas become blood. Every living creature in the seas dies.
3	Rivers to blood, all water life dies	The remaining water in the rivers, lakes, and streams turn to blood. Every creature in water dies.
4	The sun scorches the earth	Men are scorched with great heat, and still blaspheme God and refuse to repent of their sins.
5	Beast's kingdom is darkened	Every area of land claimed by the Beast is covered in darkness. Men gnaw their tongues from pain.
6	The Euphrates River runs dry	It dries that so China, India, and other eastern nations make their way to battle Jerusalem in the campaign of Armageddon (Zechariah 14).
7	"It is Finished"	Storms and the largest earthquake ever. Babylon is destroyed.

The Precursor of Armageddon

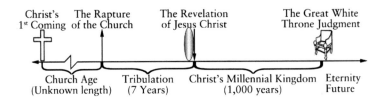

Back to Babylon

This war has been in the works for 4,500 years. After the Flood, the great grandson of Noah (Nimrod) went to a location on the shore of the Euphrates River in the plains of Shinar to a place called Babel (referring also to Babylon).

> Genesis 10:10, *"And the beginning of his kingdom was Babel, and Erech, and Accad, and Calneh, in the land of Shinar."*

"Babel" or "Babylon" is used over 350 times in the Bible, referring to a location that was at one time the headquarters for the one-world government and one-world religion that Nimrod established 4,500 years ago.

Nimrod established the one-world government. He built a city and, of course, he was the king. Genesis 10:10 says that was the beginning of his kingdom. Now you are not able to have a kingdom unless you are a king. So he was the one-world ruler of a one-world government that was headquartered in the city of Babylon. That was 4,500 years ago.

Babylon comes back into focus again during the times of Daniel and Ezekiel around 605 B.C. Nebuchadnezzar becomes the king of Babylon and the head of the Babylonian Empire. He takes Daniel and his three Hebrew buddies into Babylon to train them in the way of the Chaldeans. That begins the times of the Gentiles and the Babylonian captivity for the Jewish people.

King Nebuchadnezzar sends his mighty Babylonian army back into Jerusalem in 597 B.C., when he takes Ezekiel and about 10,000 Jews also into the Babylonian captivity. In 586 B.C., Nebuchadnezzar and his army take a third trip to Jerusalem. They destroy the city of Jerusalem and the Jewish Temple, and they take the rest of the Jews into the Babylonian captivity. The Jews will remain there for a 70-year period. The reason for that is the Jewish people failed to give rest to the land. God had told them in Leviticus 25 to rest the land every 7 years. They had not done it for 490 years (2 Chronicles 36), so God then allows the Babylonians to take the Jews out of the land for 70 years. This gave the Sabbath rest to the land for that 490-year period in which they had ignored the rest commandment.

Daniel 5 records the fall of the Babylonian Empire. Belshazzar, grandson of Nebuchadnezzar, has come to power. He is having a great big party for many of his cronies – about 1,000 of his best friends, plus their wives and concubines. They are in a drunken party in the palace there in Babylon when Belshazzar calls for those implements that were used for the sacrificial system and the worship at the Temple in Jerusalem. His grandfather, Nebuchadnezzar, had brought them into the Babylon captivity and placed most of them in the Babylon temples. Some were left in the castle, and so he calls for these vessels to be used to put their liquor in as they continued their drunken party. It was that night that the Medes and the Persians would then defeat the Babylonians.

Babylon was an impregnable city. It had two walls around it, and between the two walls was a moat filled with water and alligators. The two walls were at least 300 feet high (that's as high as a football field is long). They were each wide enough that two chariots could race around the tops of the walls, and measured a total of 9 miles long. There were, according to the ancient reports, some 250 watch towers. The city had an endless water supply, thanks to the Euphrates River flow ing underneath the northern wall and out the southern wall, and enough food to feed everyone in its walls for at least 20 days.

While the party was going on inside, the Medes and Persians decided that they could not climb the outer wall, swim the moat, climb the inner wall, and then come down into the city to defeat the Babylonians. So the Medes went north and dammed up the Euphrates, which basically opened up a tunnel underneath the walls at the northern end. The Persians went south. They dammed up the Euphrates, and it opened up a tunnel at the southern walls of this city of Babylon. Then they simply walked right in. The handwriting was on the wall. Belshazzar was tried, measured, and found wanting. Belshazzar was killed, the Babylonians were defeated, and the Babylonian Empire came to an end that night.

The City of Babylon – Alive and Well

That, indeed, was the end of the Babylonian Empire, but not the city of Babylon. Ezra 7 tells us that 75 years after the fall of the Babylonian Empire, Ezra the scribe was living in the city of Babylon. Ezra was living in that city when he was called to go into Jerusalem to reinstitute the temple practices in the Temple.

Secular history records that 200 years after the fall of the Babylonian Empire there was a man named Alexander the Great. At 32 years of age he defeated the Medo-Persian Empire, became the king of the world, the leader of the Grecian Empire, and was headquartered in the city of Babylon. It was still a strong, fortified city 200 years after the fall of the Babylonian Empire. In fact, Alexander the Great would open up the Euphrates River so that 500 gun ships could make their way out of the Persian Gulf, and up the Euphrates River to Babylon. That was two centuries after the fall of the Babylonian Empire.

Peter was on the Mount of Olives when Jesus Christ told his disciples: Start here in Jerusalem; go to Judea and Samaria, and to the uttermost parts of the earth. Peter did preach in Jerusalem on the day of Pentecost. He went to Judea and Samaria, and then he started out for the uttermost parts of the earth.

> 1 Peter 5:13, *"The church that is at Babylon, elected together with you, saluteth you; and so doth Marcus my son."*

Peter had actually gone to Babylon. Most likely he established the church there. If not, he was a guest preacher at the church, and he said all the saints salute you who are in the church here in Babylon. So Babylon was still a viable city in the first century. In the days of Peter, Babylon was the second most populated Jewish city in the world, second only to the city of Jerusalem. That would be about 500 years after the fall of the Babylonian Empire. Babylon was still alive and well at that time.

I could introduce to you a man who is a participant on our weekly radio broadcast, Prophecy Today, a nationwide hour-and-a-half call-in talk program. His name is Lt. Col. Robert Maginnis. He is an advisor to the Defense Department in Washington, D.C. He has been in modern day Babylon. There is a military base that has been there for the last several years during the war in Iraq. It is called Camp Babylon. It was the headquarters of a 21-nation multinational Peace Force headed up by the Polish military leaders. If you watch CNN or Fox News, you knew that it was a viable city because you saw it there. Geraldo Rivera on Fox News did a live telecast from Babylon. Babylon is alive and well. It is about 58 miles southwest of modern day Baghdad, Iraq. The Prime Minister of the country comes from a suburb of the city of Babylon. The city of Babylon has never been destroyed.

The Bible tells us in Isaiah 13-14 and Jeremiah 50-52, that the city of Babylon will be destroyed. The truth is Babylon has not been destroyed – that is, not yet.

> Jeremiah 50:1, 13, 39, *"The word that the LORD spake against Babylon and against the land of the Chaldeans by Jeremiah the prophet.... Because of the wrath of the LORD it shall not be inhabited, but it shall be wholly desolate: every one that goeth by Babylon shall be astonished, and hiss at all her plagues.... Therefore the wild beasts of the desert with the wild beasts of the islands shall dwell there, and the owls shall dwell therein: and it shall be no more inhabited for ever; neither shall it be dwelt in from generation to generation."*

Now the Hebrew word translated into our English word "forever" in this passage is the Hebrew word olam. It is the same word that is connected with the name of God, "elolam." This speaks of God and His eternality. The everlasting God. When you take "olam" away from "el" it still speaks of eternality. Therefore, the translation of "olam" (forever) speaks of eternality. The text tells us that Babylon will be no longer inhabited "forever," neither shall anyone dwell in it from generation to generation.

Jeremiah 50:40, *"As God overthrew Sodom and Gomorrah and the neighbour cities thereof, saith the LORD; so shall no man abide there, neither shall any son of man dwell therein."*

Jeremiah 51:29, 37, 43, *"And the land shall tremble and sorrow: for every purpose of the LORD shall be performed against Babylon, to make the land of Babylon a desolation without an inhabitant.... And Babylon shall become heaps, a dwellingplace for dragons, an astonishment, and an hissing, without an inhabitant.... Her cities are a desolation, a dry land, and a wilderness, a land wherein no man dwelleth, neither doth any son of man pass thereby."*

Those are just a few of the verses in Jeremiah 50-51 referring to Babylon's destruction. Babylonians desecrated those implements that had been taken from the Jewish Temple in Jerusalem. Because of His Temple, God is going to bring judgment upon the city of Babylon. Many other passages of Scripture talk about Babylon being completely destroyed, devastated, and never to have inhabitants live in it again. That has not yet happened. These prophecies have never been fulfilled. But for that to happen, Babylon will once again have to rise to prominence.

Revelation: A Chronology

Dr. Jimmy DeYoung

REVELATION: A CHRONOLOGY   DR. JIMMY DEYOUNG

THE LAST HALF OF THE TRIBULATION

The Two Babylons

Revelation 18:1-2, *"And after these things I saw another angel come down from heaven, having great power; and the earth was lightened with his glory. And he cried mightily with a strong voice, saying, Babylon the great is fallen, is fallen, and is become the habitation of devils, and the hold of every foul spirit, and a cage of every unclean and hateful bird."*

Here we see the fulfillment of all those prophecies against Babylon. May I submit that this is talking about the literal city of Babylon – and is a completely different event than the described destruction of the woman called "Babylon the great, mother of harlots" in Revelation 17.

Revelation 17

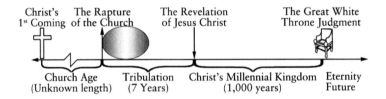

Revelation 17 is talking about a woman, a mother, a prostitute, a whore. Those terms are used a total of 10 times in the chapter, and the word "her" 9 times, all referring to a false church a total of 19 times. Revelation 18 is talking about a city. The word "Babylon" is used 3 times and the word "city" is used 7 times; so 10 times it is referring to a city that, I would suggest, is the literal city of Babylon. Chapter 17 refers to a religious system. Chapter 18 refers to a governmental, economic, political system. In chapter 17, when they destroy Babylon, nobody cries. Nobody is upset about it at all. In fact, they were happy to do it. However, in chapter 18, when Babylon is destroyed, all those who have grown rich because of Babylon are very sorrowful and mournful, even crying.

Revelation 18:8-10, *"Therefore shall her plagues come in one day, death, and mourning, and famine; and she shall be utterly burned with fire: for strong is the Lord God who judgeth her. And the kings of the earth, who have committed fornication and lived deliciously with her, shall bewail her, and lament for her, when they shall see the smoke of her burning, Standing afar off for the fear of her torment, saying, Alas, alas that great city Babylon, that mighty city! for in one hour is thy judgment come."*

Revelation 18

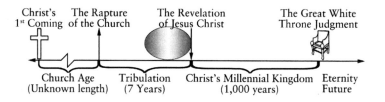

Babylon is a literal city that will be the headquarters for the Antichrist who will rule over the one-world economic, political, and governmental system.

After the false religion (the ecclesiastical Babylon of chapter 17) is destroyed, the Antichrist leaves the seven-hilled city of Rome. He goes to Jerusalem (2 Thessalonians 2:4). He enters the Temple and claims to be God. This is the Abomination of Desolation. He disgraces the Temple. He desecrates the Temple. The Abomination of Desolation talked about in Daniel 11 will take place at the midpoint of the Tribulation.

At that time, the False Prophet will put a statue in the Holy of Holies and perform lying signs, wonders, and miracles to cause the world to worship the image of the beast. That is the time when "mark of the beast" will be put on people's foreheads or the back of their hands. If you are going to buy or sell, you must have the mark of the Antichrist.

The Antichrist leaves Jerusalem. The statue of the Antichrist is there in the Temple. That is good enough for him. He goes into Babylon and sets up this one-world economic, political, and governmental system. From out of Babylon, literal Babylon, he will be head-quartered for the last 3½ years of the Tribulation.

> Revelation 18:17-19, *"For in one hour so great riches is come to nought. And every shipmaster, and all the company in ships, and sailors, and as many as trade by sea, stood afar off, And cried when they saw the smoke of her burning, saying, What city is like unto this great city! And they cast dust on their heads, and cried, weeping and wailing, saying, Alas, alas that great city, wherein were made rich all that had ships in the sea by reason of her costliness! for in one hour is she made desolate."*

The Last of the 21 Judgments

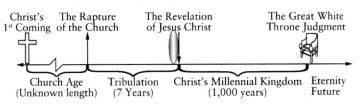

There are Seven Seal Judgments, Seven Trumpets Judgments, and Seven Vial Judgments. Let's look at the last of these twenty-one judgments, which will be the physical cause of the destruction of the city of Babylon.

130

The Seventh Vial Judgment, Revelation 16:17-18, *"And the seventh angel poured out his vial into the air; and there came a great voice out of the temple of heaven, from the throne, saying, It is done. And there were voices, and thunders, and lightnings; and there was a great earthquake, such as was not since men were upon the earth, so mighty an earthquake, and so great."*

This will be the most powerful earthquake to ever hit the earth. It will, among other things, destroy the city of Babylon.

Revelation 16:19, *"And the great city was divided into three parts, and the cities of the nations fell: and great Babylon came in remembrance before God, to give unto her the cup of the wine of the fierceness of his wrath."*

Because the Babylonians desecrated the implements used in the Temple to worship and to offer sacrifice unto God, judgment is going to fall heavily upon them.

Revelation 16:20-21, *"And every island fled away, and the mountains were not found. And there fell upon men a great hail out of heaven, every stone about the weight of a talent: and men blasphemed God because of the plague of the hail; for the plague thereof was exceeding great."*

The definition of the weight of a talent has a variance in opinion. Some say about 50 pounds. Some say about 100 pounds. Let's say 75 pounds, to compromise between the two figures. Can you imagine a piece of hail weighing 75 pounds? That's what will fall upon Babylon, and it will destroy the city.

Israeli Prime Minister Benjamin Netanyahu said that the Iraqis are installing the latest cutting edge, state-of-the-art telecommunications system that will give them a capability of communicating across the world. Netanyahu said it could well become the Silicon Valley of not only the Middle East, but the entire world.

Iraq is the second largest source of oil in the entire world, second only to Saudi Arabia. Financial Times reports that, according to some petroleum engineers, Saudi Arabia is going to run out of oil in about 10 years, which could then make the Iraqi oil supply (of which they have only used up 2 percent) the greatest source for oil in the world. And it would make Iraq one of the richest nations – if not the richest nation – in the world. We can see that the stage is being set for Bible prophecy to play out just like it is called for by the ancient Jewish prophets. Babylon will be the headquarters for the Antichrist. It will be destroyed by Jesus Christ Himself. Satan, the Antichrist, and the False Prophet will flee to Jerusalem to gather the armies of the world to take on the return of Jesus Christ.

The Campaign of Armageddon

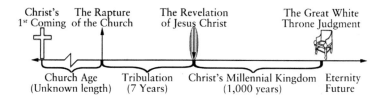

Remember, 2 Peter 1:20 tells us that there is no prophecy in the Scriptures of private interpretation. What that means is that all the prophecies in the Word of God are coordinated. They fit together like a hand in a glove. They cannot contradict each other.

There is a reason for this coordination. The Holy Spirit of God breathed into these ancient Jewish prophets exactly what He wanted them to write. So really, there is only one Author with many scribes.

These various books by different human authors all tell one solid, cohesive story. So we must come to a conclusion on how everything is going to play out, and what the scenario is for the campaign of Armageddon by going to a number of Scriptures.

Zechariah 14:1, "*Behold, the day of the LORD cometh, and thy spoil shall be divided in the midst of thee.*"

The "Day of the Lord" is defined as any time in history when God intercedes in the affairs of man personally upon the earth. That term can be generally applied to the 7-year Tribulation Period, the Second Coming of

133

Jesus Christ, and the 1000-year Millennial Kingdom. However, the specific usage, as we see right here in Zechariah 14, is the day that Jesus Christ comes back to the earth.

> Zechariah 14:2, "For I will gather all nations against Jerusalem to battle; and the city shall be taken, and the houses rifled, and the women ravished; and half of the city shall go forth into captivity, and the residue of the people shall not be cut off from the city."

All the armies of the world will be gathered at Jerusalem.

Where is the USA in Bible Prophecy?

I was in a "Prophecy Q&A session" in a church recently and I was asked, "Where is the USA in Bible prophecy?" This question happens to be my most often-asked question in these Q&A sessions.

Before I could answer, somebody in the back said, "Hey, I know!"

"Okay, sir," I said. "Where?"

He said, "Jerusalem."

I said, "How do you get that?"

He said, "Very simple, J e r - U S A - l e m."

There was a chuckle across the entire congregation as the man gave his explanation of how the United States was in Bible prophecy, but in essence, he was correct. Look at Zechariah 14:2, "For I will gather all nations against Jerusalem."

Should, after seven years of judgment, there be any remnant of the United States, they will be gathered at Jerusalem. This is the only reference in Bible prophecy to the United States.

My personal opinion is that at the Rapture of the Church, the backbone of this nation (born-again believers) will leave this world and this Super Power nation will become a powerless nation. Any nation that sins the way America has sinned, God is going to have to judge.

I believe there are two reasons that God has not judged America already. First, because America is the launch pad for world evangelization. The money, the manpower, and the materials come out of America and reach around the world. The second reason is that the United States has protected the Jewish people.

When you take the body of Christ out at the Rapture, America will become a shell of a nation. It will no longer protect the Jewish people. We see that already beginning to happen even while we are still here.

The Armies Gather at Jerusalem

So all the armies of the world gather at Jerusalem according to Zechariah 14. How many people would that be? I am going to be very conservative in my estimate. There are 192 members of the United Nations, but depending on which way the political winds are blowing when you ask the question, the number of countries in the world can range between 168 and 254.

135

Let's take about half of the average of those numbers. Let's say that 100 nations gather, and let's say that each nation had a militia, an army, of about 1 million soldiers. So that would be 100 million soldiers that will gather with Antichrist, Satan, and the False Prophet at the city of Jerusalem to take on the returning Jesus Christ.

> Zechariah 14:3, *"Then shall the LORD go forth, and fight against those nations, as when he fought in the day of battle."*

> Revelation 19:11-13, *"And I saw heaven opened, and behold a white horse; and he that sat upon him was called Faithful and True, and in righteousness he doth judge and make war. His eyes were as a flame of fire, and on his head were many crowns; and he had a name written, that no man knew, but he himself. And he was clothed with a vesture dipped in blood: and his name is called The Word of God."*

Of course we are talking about Jesus Christ. This description found here in Revelation 19 is very similar to the description of the glorified, resurrected Jesus Christ in Revelation chapter 1.

> Revelation 19:14, *"And the armies which were in heaven followed him upon white horses, clothed in fine linen, white and clean."*

Jesus Christ gets on a white horse (and I believe He will literally be on a horse). We, the Church, the bride of Christ, who have been married to Christ going through that 7-year celebration of the Marriage Supper of the Lamb, will join Jesus Christ. We will get on these white horses and we will come back to the earth. The heavens open up, and He starts back to the earth.

The Layout of the Battleground

> Zechariah 14:4-5, *"And his feet shall stand in that day upon the mount of Olives, which is before Jerusalem on the east, and the mount of Olives shall cleave in the midst thereof toward the east and toward the west, and there shall be a very great valley; and half of the mountain shall remove toward the north, and half of it toward the south. And ye shall flee to the valley of the mountains; for the valley of the mountains shall reach unto Azal: yea, ye shall flee, like as ye fled from before the earthquake in the days of Uzziah king of Judah: and the LORD my God shall come, and all the saints with thee."*

Who was the "ye" referring to here? It is not referring to the Jews. They will rush to Jesus Christ, their Messiah. It is referring to those who have gathered under the auspices of Satan, Antichrist, and False Prophet. These 100 million soldiers from the nations of the world have gathered in Jerusalem for the beginning of the campaign of Armageddon. They will flee to the valley of the mountains.

If you have never been to the Jezreel Valley (we would love to take you there on one of our tours to Israel), you would not be familiar with the fact that the Jezreel Valley is approximately 1,000 square miles. It is

14 miles wide, some 67 miles long, and is situated among the mountains. Over to the West is Mount Carmel, up to the North are the mountains of Nazareth, out to the East is Mount Moreh and Mount Tabor, and there are the other mountains to the east. Going down to the Jordan Valley you have Mount Gilboa where Saul and his sons were killed, and then you have the mountains going back south to Jerusalem, the mountains of Samaria. Many mountains surround this 1,000 square mile valley.

Napoleon, who was a great military strategist, said that when he fought on the Jezreel Valley it was the most strategic battlefield in all the earth. He said that the armies could fight in this large area, this surface of the valley, and then in the evening they could go up and bivouac on the slopes of the mountain, regroup to come again, and fight the next day.

These people who have gathered in Jerusalem under the leadership of Satan, Antichrist, and False Prophet are going to make their way toward the valley of the mountains. What is Jesus going to do? The Bible tells us in the book of Ezekiel and the book of Zechariah that Jesus Christ is going to reshape Jerusalem.

Zechariah 14:10, *"All the land shall be turned as a plain from Geba to Rimmon south of Jerusalem: and it shall be lifted up, and inhabited in her place, from Benjamin's gate unto the place of the first gate, unto the corner gate, and from the tower of Hananeel unto the king's winepresses."*

What is going to happen is that the city of Jerusalem, which is about 8½ square miles, is going to be lifted up. Ezekiel explains that after it is reformed, Jerusalem will be about 2,500 square miles, 50 miles on each side. The state of Israel is about 70 miles wide from the Mediterranean coast to the Jordan River. Jerusalem is going to be almost the entire width of the state of Israel. Ezekiel also tells us that the Temple Mount, which will be about 1 square mile, will be lifted up above the city of Jerusalem and that Jesus Christ (Zechariah 6:12) will build his Temple, the Temple that is described in Ezekiel 40-46. There are 202 verses that give detailed information about the Messiah's Temple.

That is what Jesus Christ is going to be doing during that time when the people, the enemies of Jesus Christ, those compatriots of Satan, Antichrist, and False Prophet, make their way to the Jezreel Valley for this battle of Armageddon.

> Revelation 19:15-16, *"And out of his mouth goeth a sharp sword, that with it he should smite the nations: and he shall rule them with a rod of iron: and he treadeth the winepress of the fierceness and wrath of Almighty God. And he hath on his vesture and on his thigh a name written, KING OF KINGS, AND LORD OF LORDS."*

This is now talking about the actual battle of Armageddon; the campaign of Armageddon will include the battle of Armageddon.

> Revelation 14:19-20, *"And the angel thrust in his sickle into the earth, and gathered the vine of the earth, and cast it into the great winepress of the wrath of God. And the winepress was trodden without the city, and blood came out of the winepress, even unto the horse bridles, by the space of a thousand and six hundred furlongs."*

The city spoken of here is Jerusalem. Sixteen-hundred furlongs is about 176 miles. The blood is going to fl ow out of the bodies of the animals and the men who come to the battle of Armageddon, and this blood will flow out about as high as the horses' bridles for 176 miles.

One Sabbath day during His earthly ministry, Jesus Christ was in the synagogue in Nazareth. He read Isaiah 61:1 and then half of verse 2. Here is the portion He read:

> Isaiah 61:1-2a, *"The Spirit of the Lord GOD is upon me; because the LORD hath anointed me to preach good tidings unto the meek; he hath sent me to bind up the brokenhearted, to proclaim liberty to the captives, and the opening of the prison to them that are bound; To proclaim the acceptable year of the LORD,"*

At that time, Jesus closed the book! Even though there were not chapter and verse divisions in the Bible at the time of Christ's reading that day, it was still an unusual place to stop since it is the middle of a sentence and in the middle of a couplet. Let's see what the rest of that verse says.

> Isaiah 61:2b, "...*and the day of vengeance of our God; to comfort all that mourn.*"

He did not read that portion that day there in the synagogue in Nazareth. Jesus was not there at that time to fulfill that part of the prophecy, that has yet to take place.

Nazareth overlooks the Jezreel Valley. I can just imagine when Jesus Christ was young He would have spent time on the slopes of Nazareth looking into the Jezreel Valley. He would not start His public ministry until He was 30, so that gave Him a good number of years in Nazareth to be able to look out there, contemplating what was going to happen in that Jezreel Valley below. One day He, Jesus Christ, will bring forth the wrath of God.

Christ Returns as Victorious King

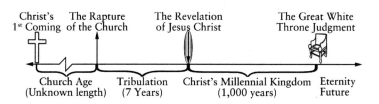

There are two rhetorical questions asked in Isaiah 63 that will be answered by Jesus Christ himself.

Isaiah 63:1a, *"Who is this that cometh from Edom, with dyed garments from Bozrah? this that is glorious in his apparel, travelling in the greatness of his strength?"*

The first question asked is, "who is coming out of Edom with dyed garments from Bozrah?" Edom is the lower part of modern-day Jordan. Bozrah is at the entrance to the headquartered city of Edom, the impregnable city of Petra. Petra, I believe, has been prepared by God (Revelation 12:6) to protect the Jewish people in the last half of the Tribulation.

Sadly, two out of every three Jews that enter into the Tribulation Period will be killed during that terrible time of judgment (Zechariah 13:8). But that also means that one-third will be protected. Not only will they survive the Tribulation with their physical lives intact, but they will turn to Jesus Christ as their Lord and Savior. I believe that it is in Petra that this third will be protected.

Isaiah asks the rhetorical question, "who comes from Edom?" Jesus Christ gives the answer.

Isaiah 63:1b, *"I that speak in righteousness, mighty to save."*

Now, the second of Isaiah's rhetorical questions.

Isaiah 63:2, *"Wherefore art thou red in thine apparel, and thy garments like him that treadeth in the winefat?"*

Remember, Revelation 14:19-20 speaks about blood flowing out of the great winepress of the wrath of God for 1,600 furlongs.

> Isaiah 63:3-4, *"I have trodden the winepress alone; and of the people there was none with me: for I will tread them in mine anger, and trample them in my fury; and their blood shall be sprinkled upon my garments, and I will stain all my raiment. For the day of vengeance is in mine heart, and the year of my redeemed is come."*

Jesus Christ is the One who will tread the winepress with the fierceness of the wrath of almighty God. The blood will flow out of the bodies of the animals and the men in that battle of Armageddon there in the Jezreel Valley.

I mentioned that my conservative estimate is that there would be around 100 different countries gathered there with maybe a total of 100 million people ready to fight. That is just my estimate, there is no figure in the Scripture that gives us that number.

One-hundred-million soldiers would have 600 million quarts of blood. The blood has to flow 176 miles, about as high as the horses' bridles. If you look it up, you'll be able to see this will be a valley of blood extending about 50 quarts per foot for 176 miles. That's about as high as a horse's bridle. I believe that these passages of Scripture are literal and should be taken as such.

From the Jezreel Valley to the entrance of Petra, is approximately 176 miles. Jesus Christ walks all the way from the battlefield of Armageddon, He goes over into Petra, He gathers up those Jews whom He has protected for the past 3½ years, and He brings them into Jerusalem.

> Ezekiel 43:1-2, "*Afterward he brought me to the gate, even the gate that looketh toward the east: And, behold, the glory of the God of Israel came from the way of the east: and his voice was like a noise of many waters: and the earth shined with his glory.*"

The gate that looks toward the East is, of course, what we call the "Eastern Gate" today.

Isn't it interesting? Here we read about a voice of many waters, just like in Revelation 1:15, 14:2, and 19:6.

> Ezekiel 43:4, 7, "*And the glory of the LORD came into the house by the way of the gate whose prospect is toward the east.... And he said unto me, Son of man, the place of my throne, and the place of the soles of my feet, where I will dwell in the midst of the children of Israel for ever, and my holy name, shall the house of Israel no more defile, neither they, nor their kings, by their whoredom, nor by the carcases of their kings in their high places.*"

The "place of my throne" would be the Holy of Holies in the Temple that Jesus Christ will build while all of those soldiers make their way up to the Jezreel

144

Valley. Jesus Christ goes into the Holy of Holies and sets up his kingdom in the city of Jerusalem which concludes this campaign of Armageddon.

The armies gather in Jerusalem to take on Jesus Christ (Zechariah 14) as He returns with us out of Heaven. He steps back onto the slopes of the Mount of Olives. The heavens open up and Christ comes out (Revelation 19:11). The Jews are under attack. All of Jerusalem is surrounded and is being destroyed, then Jesus Christ the Messiah returns. He defeats the enemies that are there in Jerusalem.

The survivors will make their way up the valley all the way (about 97 miles) to the Jezreel Valley. Meanwhile, Jesus will build His Temple in Jerusalem (Zechariah 6:12). He establishes Jerusalem as the center focus of the state of Israel. The city becomes 2,500 square miles and is lifted up. The Temple Mount, a square mile, is also lifted up. Then Christ, the Creator God, who is also Jesus, a human carpenter, builds His 21-story tall Temple on top of that new mountain on top of that massive new plateau.

Jesus Christ then goes to the Jezreel Valley. He opens His mouth and out comes that sharp two-edged sword, and He casts the people dead. Then the blood flows as high as the horses' bridles for 176 miles and Jesus walks though that valley of blood from the Jezreel Valley all the way to Petra.

He gathers His people, brings them back into the city of Jerusalem and up onto the Temple Mount. He

145

then goes into the Holy of Holies and establishes His kingdom.

The Jewish Feasts and the Day of Atonement

Think about this: all seven Jewish feasts (Leviticus 23) have already been or will be fulfilled by Jesus Christ. The first four feasts, the feasts of the springtime, have been fulfilled by Jesus Christ.

He was crucified on Passover, he was buried on Unleavened Bread, then on First Fruits, Jesus Christ resurrected from the dead, and 50 days after First Fruits, as Jesus promised, the Holy Spirit came.

In the proper day sequences, Jesus Christ fulfilled those fi rst four feasts, the spring feasts. It is logical, then, that Jesus Christ will fulfill the last three feasts, the fall feasts, and do it in the proper day sequences.

He will come back on the Feast of Trumpets – Rosh Hashanah. Now that's not the Rapture of the Church. This feast has nothing to do with the Rapture. This is the Second Coming that is pictured by Rosh Hashanah, the Feast of Trumpets.

> Matthew 24:31, *"And he shall send his angels with a great sound of a trumpet, and they shall gather together his elect from the four winds, from one end of heaven to the other."*

When Jesus Christ comes back to the earth, He turns to the angel and says blow the trumpet to call a solemn assembly. Jesus Christ returns to the earth at the end of the Tribulation on Rosh Hashanah, the feast of trumpets.

Between Rosh Hashanah and Yom Kippur, the Day of Atonement, is a 10-day period, called the Ten Awesome Days. That does not mean awesome like fantastic or wonderful, it means being full of awe, it is actually a solemn time of personal reflection for the Jewish people.

It will be during that time, that Jesus will reconstruct the city of Jerusalem, reconstruct the Temple Mount, and then construct His Temple. This will take place while these armies of Satan, Antichrist, and False Prophet make their way some 90 miles up to the Jezreel Valley to prepare for the mother of all battles, the battle of Armageddon.

Jesus Christ will go up to that location, He will speak, they will all die, the blood flows as high as the horses' bridles for 176 miles (over to Petra), He goes to Petra, and He gathers in those Jewish survivors (the one-third of all the Jews who entered into the Tribulation – that would be about 4 million using today's figures). Jesus then brings them into Jerusalem through the Eastern Gate, walking into the Holy of Holies and sitting down. The day that Christ enters the Holy of Holies is Yom Kippur; it's the Day of Atonement.

According to Hebrews 6:20 and 7:17, Jesus is the great High Priest, not after the order of Levi or Aaron, but after the order of Melchizedek. Jesus Christ is the

High Priest and He goes into the Holy of Holies on Yom Kippur.

Hebrews 9:24-28 says that, in the past, the high priest would go into the Temple and into the Holy of Holies every year on Yom Kippur. It continues on to say that now, in the end of days, Jesus Christ goes into the Holy of Holies. He has already gone into the original Holy of Holies which resides in the Temple in Heaven. Now, at the end of the Tribulation, Jesus Christ will go into the Holy of Holies for the very first time on earth.

The Feast of Passover was for individual salvation. The Day of Atonement, Yom Kippur, was for a national salvation. Zechariah 3:9 promises that at this time, after Christ has gathered all the remaining Jews in the world to Jerusalem, all of Israel shall be saved in a day. That day will be Yom Kippur, the Day of Atonement.

There will be four days of judgment. Judgment of the living Jews, judgment of the living Gentiles, judgment of the resurrected Jews, and judgment of Satan, Antichrist, and False Prophet. After those four days of judgment, the Millennial Kingdom begins on the day of the Feast of Tabernacles. Jesus Christ will fulfill all seven of the Jewish feast days in the proper day sequences.

Revelation: A Chronology — Dr. Jimmy DeYoung

THE POSTLUDE TO THE TRIBULATION

The Millennial Reign of Christ

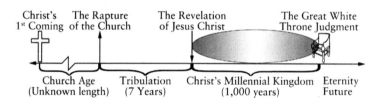

Satan is Bound

Revelation 20:1-3, *"And I saw an angel come down from heaven, having the key of the bottomless pit and a great chain in his hand. And he laid hold on the dragon, that old serpent, which is the Devil, and Satan, and bound him a thousand years, And cast him into the bottomless pit, and shut him up, and set a seal upon him, that he should deceive the nations no more, till the thousand years should be fulfilled: and after that he must be loosed a little season."*

This is going to be the very first time in history that Satan is going to be bound. You remember Satan was originally known as Lucifer, the most prominent of all the angels created by God. God placed Lucifer over all of creation. Lucifer chose to rebel against God. From the time of the fall of man (Genesis 3), until the beginning of Christ's Millennial Kingdom (Revelation 20), the world has been under the rule of Satan, a Satanocracy, not a theocracy, which is under the rule of God.

That means that everything described in the entire Bible except for the first three chapters and the last three chapters has or will occur in a world under the control of Satan.

Since the moment he was created, and from the moment he rebelled, Satan has never once been bound. There are many people out there talking about binding Satan. That is not the case. There is no way anybody will bind Satan.

The little book of Jude, which is right before the book of Revelation, says that Michael the archangel would not dare to tell Satan what to do.

> Jude 9, "Yet Michael the archangel, when contending with the devil he disputed about the body of Moses, durst not bring against him a railing accusation, but said, The Lord rebuke thee."

Even Michael the archangel, who is much more powerful than we mere humans, would not confront Satan. Nobody has ever bound Satan.

In 1 Peter 5:8, we read that Satan is like a roaring lion, roaming around the world and devouring whomever he will.

Satan has not been bound, he is not bound right now, and he will not be bound until the time of the beginning of the Millennial Kingdom, when Jesus Christ dispatches an angel to chain up Satan and cast him in the Bottomless Pit for 1,000 years.

The Bible does not give us information about the location of the Bottomless Pit. I would suggest it might be one of those black holes in outer space someplace that we don't know much about. Wherever that pit may be, Satan will be bound there during the Millennial Reign of Christ.

How do we relate to Satan if we do not bind him? James tells us exactly what to do.

> James 4:7-8a, *"Submit yourselves therefore to God. Resist the devil, and he will flee from you. Draw nigh to God, and he will draw nigh to you."*

We draw close to God in submission and resist the Devil, and that will send the Devil running. Satan is going to continue to be active all the way up to the beginning of the Millennial Kingdom. At that time, he will be bound for 1,000, years only to be loosed at the end.

The Promise of the Kingdom

Revelation 20:4, *"And I saw thrones, and they sat upon them, and judgment was given unto them: and I saw the souls of them that were beheaded for the witness of Jesus, and for the word of God, and which had not worshipped the beast, neither his image, neither had received his mark upon their foreheads, or in their hands; and they lived and reigned with Christ a thousand years."*

Here we see the promise of the 1,000-year Kingdom period, the Millennium. The Old Testament Jewish prophets often spoke about the promise of a Kingdom, but the length of 1,000 years was not necessarily mentioned until this passage.

During the earthly ministry of Christ, John the Baptist was preaching the "gospel of the kingdom." When John the Baptist saw Christ on the banks of the Jordan River his response was, "Repent ye: for the kingdom of heaven is at hand" (Matthew 3:2).

The truth is, when Jesus came, He offered the kingdom to the Jewish people, right then and there. They rejected John's message, they rejected John (who was the Elijah who could have come), and they rejected Jesus Christ who had come to set up the kingdom. Thus, the kingdom was delayed from being implemented on the earth. But the kingdom will indeed come as promised by the prophecy that God gave to Daniel.

Daniel is about 70 years of age at the time recorded in Daniel 7. He had a dream one night, and this is what he saw.

> Daniel 7:13-14, *"I saw in the night visions, and, behold, one like the Son of man came with the clouds of heaven, and came to the Ancient of days, and they brought him near before him. And there was given him dominion, and glory, and a kingdom, that all people, nations, and languages, should serve him: his dominion is an everlasting dominion, which shall not pass away, and his kingdom that which shall not be destroyed."*

The "Son of man" would be Jesus Christ. The "Ancient of days" would be God the Father. Jesus Christ will be given dominion, glory, and an everlasting kingdom over all people. That word "everlasting" is olam, which again is connected with Elolam, the name of God which speaks of the eternality of God. So we see Jesus' Kingdom in Daniel's vision.

It is also foretold in Daniel 2. This time through Nebuchadnezzar's dream, which Daniel interpreted. This is a blessed prophecy and a great promise!

He talked about the 10 toes of iron and clay, similar to the 10 horns of Daniel 7, both visions referring to the Revived Roman Empire.

> Daniel 2:44, *"And in the days of these kings* [the Revived Roman Empire] *shall the God of heaven set up a kingdom, which shall never be destroyed: and the kingdom shall not be left to*

155

other people, but it shall break in pieces and consume all these kingdoms, and it shall stand for ever."

The earthly kingdom will last for 1,000 years, but Jesus Christ's kingdom will go on forever and ever into Eternity Future.

The People of the Kingdom

The people of the kingdom will be those who are alive upon the earth at the end of the Tribulation and their offspring. These will be both Jews and Gentiles.

Matthew 25 is a continuation of the Olivet Discourse. After Jesus Christ describes the time leading up to His Second Coming, He talks about the judgment for the Jewish people who live through the entire Tribulation Period, as well as the Gentile people who live through the entire Tribulation Period. There will be those at the end of the 7 years who have survived; the ones who know Jesus Christ as their Messiah will enter into the Millennial Kingdom with physical bodies.

Jesus shares the parable of the ten virgins (Matthew 25:1-13), which is a judgment of the Jewish people. There were five who had oil in their lamps and there were five who were not prepared to go out to meet the bridegroom because they had no oil in their lamps.

The bridegroom says to those five without oil, "I know you not" (Matthew 25:12). That is the judgment of the Jews who are alive at the end of the Tribulation. And those who have trusted Messiah, Jesus Christ as their Lord and Savior, enter into the kingdom period with physical bodies.

Also in Matthew 25 (verses 31-46), it talks about the judgment of the sheep and the goats. That would be the judgment for the living Gentiles. The sheep would be those who know Jesus Christ as Lord and Savior, and they prove that by serving the Jewish people, the brethren of Jesus Christ.

The goats would be those lost Gentiles, who will be placed in a location to wait for the final judgment, the Great White Throne Judgment.

There will be those who enter into the Millennial Kingdom with physical bodies. Isaiah 65:20 says that they will even have children. A child will live 100 years of age and still be considered a child. At that point, if they reject Jesus Christ (who will be the head of that earthly theocracy) they will be sentenced to judgment at the Great White Throne.

The Peace of the Kingdom

What is it going to be like during that kingdom? We do know that Jesus tells us in Matthew 19:28, "...in the regeneration when the Son of Man shall sit in the throne of His glory...," it will be an earth as it was at the time of Creation. The word "regeneration" (palig-genesia in Greek) literally means "Genesis again."

The Bible doesn't tell us a whole lot of information about what the political conditions on earth will be during that Millennial Kingdom. However, we do get a few precious glimpses into life during the Kingdom.

> Isaiah 9:6, "*For unto us a child is born, unto us a son is given: and the government shall be upon his shoulder: and his name shall be called Wonderful, Counsellor, The mighty God, The everlasting Father, The Prince of Peace.*"

Often we are asked to pray for the peace of Jerusalem (Psalm 122:6). When we pray for the peace of Jerusalem, we are not praying that some politician or humanitarian will come up with a solution to the "Middle East Conflict." What we are actually praying for is for the Prince of Peace, Jesus Christ, to come back. The only true period of peace that will ever be on this earth is when Jesus Christ rules and reigns from the Temple in Jerusalem during that time known as the Millennial Kingdom.

> Isaiah 11:6-9, "*The wolf also shall dwell with the lamb, and the leopard shall lie down with the kid; and the calf and the young lion and the fatling together; and a little child shall lead them. And the cow and the bear shall feed; their young ones shall lie down together: and the lion shall eat straw like the ox. And the sucking child shall play on the hole of the asp, and the weaned child shall put his hand on the cockatrice' den. They shall not hurt nor destroy in all my holy mountain: for the earth shall be full of the knowledge of the LORD, as the waters cover the sea.*"

It is a miracle that those animals will be lying down together, without eating one another. Today if you laid a young calf next to a lion, the calf would be gone and the lion would be full. Same thing with a wolf and a sheep. But in the Millennial Kingdom, it's going to be a beautiful, beautiful time of peace on the earth as Christ will bring peace even to the animal world.

And the snakes mentioned are very venomous snakes. The "cockatrice" is probably a cobra, or maybe a viper; very poisonous. But at that time, the children will be playing with these snakes because God will change it as it was before the fall of man in the Garden of Eden.

What a blessed time it's going to be. Men are going to lay down their weapons of war, they are going to pick up their plows and cultivate this earth, and the earth is going to bring forth great fruit. It will be a marvelous time.

The Paradise of the Kingdom

In Genesis 1-3, you'll remember, Jesus Christ had His first theocracy on this earth. This was in the Garden of Eden. May I suggest to you, the Garden of Eden will once again be the location of the headquarters of Jesus Christ as He rules and reigns in His coming theocracy?

Some may point out, correctly I might add, that I just stated, several times, that Jesus Christ would be ruling and reigning from the Holy of Holies on the

Temple Mount in Jerusalem. But now I am saying that He will be ruling from the Garden of Eden. How can they both be true?

Ezekiel 28 talks about the rebellion of Lucifer against God, which doomed him to become Satan.

> Ezekiel 28:13-14, *"Thou hast been in Eden the garden of God; every precious stone was thy covering, the sardius, topaz, and the diamond, the beryl, the onyx, and the jasper, the sapphire, the emerald, and the carbuncle, and gold: the workmanship of thy tabrets and of thy pipes was prepared in thee in the day that thou wast created. Thou art the anointed cherub that covereth; and I have set thee so: thou wast upon the holy mountain of God; thou hast walked up and down in the midst of the stones of fire."*

The Garden of God at the time of creation would be the Garden of Eden. The phrase "holy mountain of God" is used 18 times in the Old Testament. It is used twice here in Ezekiel 28 as it is referring to the Garden of Eden, but throughout the rest of the Old Testament it is always used to refer to the Temple Mount in Jerusalem.

We know that by the definition given in the prayer that Daniel offered (Daniel 9:16, 19-20). Daniel is praying for "thy city Jerusalem, thy holy mountain." The holy mountain of God is the location of the Garden of Eden.

This idea may be new to many Christian scholars, but it is not new to Orthodox Jewish scholars. For thousands of years, the Jews have believed that the Temple Mount and the "foundation stone" (the stone underneath the Dome of the Rock) is where the Holy of Holies was located. It is also where the Ark of the Covenant rested in the Temple that stood on the Temple Mount and was the location where God brought into existence humankind. In other words, He created Adam there, on that "foundation stone" in Jerusalem.

Genesis 1 records the creation, Genesis 2 gives the special effects of creation, and here we find out more information about the Garden of Eden.

Genesis 2:8-15 gives some descriptions of the location of the Garden.

> Portions of Genesis 2:8-15, *"And the LORD God planted a garden eastward in Eden.... And a river went out of Eden to water the garden; and from thence it was parted, and became into four heads. The name of the first is Pison: ... the second river is Gihon: ... the third river is Hiddekel: ... And the fourth river is Euphrates. And the LORD God took the man, and put him into the garden of Eden to dress it and to keep it."*

Many people see these verses and conclude that the Garden of Eden is over near the Tigris and the Euphrates River. I don't know where we get that from because the Bible does not say that the Tigris and the Euphrates were near the original Garden of Eden.

What does the Bible say? Genesis 2:10, "And a river went out of Eden to water the garden...." That is one

river. The "river went out of Eden ,,, and from thence"
– in other words, it went from Eden to someplace else,
someplace outside of the Garden. The river left the
Garden and broke up into four different rivers.

Genesis 2:11-14 mentions the names of these four
rivers: The Pison, the Gihon, the Tigris (Hiddekel is
more often translated Tigris), and the Euphrates. Now
today, we know where the Tigris and the Euphrates are
located. They start up in Turkey and extend through
Syria, down through Iraq and Kuwait all the way into
the Persian Gulf.

Many have suggested that in Iraq is the original site
of the Garden of Eden because of the location today of
the Tigris and Euphrates. How do we know where the
Tigris and Euphrates were before the Flood?

Genesis 2 is set at the time of creation before the
Flood. After the Flood, the topography of the entire
earth was changed. We know where the Tigris and Euphrates are located today, but we really have no idea as
to where the Tigris and Euphrates might have been before the Flood took place.

What about the Pison River? Where is that located?
I do not know, but I do know where the fourth river is,
that's the Gihon River. The Gihon River comes out
from underneath the Temple Mount.

I talked with an archeologist at the city of David,
which is the original site of the city of Jerusalem. He
and his son (who is the equivalent of a Navy Seal in the
Israeli Navy) and a couple of his buddies went on an

expedition. They put on their scuba equipment and got down in the pool of Shalom, which is in the city of David and is fed by the Gihon River. They swam up underneath the Temple Mount and there they found the headwaters for the Gihon River. Remember, that's where David on his deathbed got up, told his servant to go get some water from the Gihon, and he anointed King Solomon to be the next king of Israel (I Kings 1:33). The Gihon River flows out from underneath the Temple Mount.

> Revelation 2:7b, *"To him that overcometh will I give to eat of the tree of life, which is in the midst of the paradise of God."*

During the Millennial Kingdom, the tree of life will be on the Temple Mount in Jerusalem. How will the people who enter the kingdom in physical bodies be able to sustain life physically for 1,000 years? They will eat from the tree of life.

You might remember, God told the angels to guard the entrance to the Garden of Eden (Genesis 3), because He did not want Adam and Eve, then in sin, to get into the Garden and eat of the tree of life. That would curse them to live forever in their sin.

THE END OF THE 1,000 YEARS

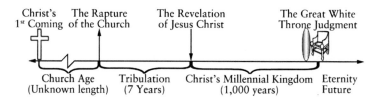

Christ's   The Rapture   The Revelation   The Great White
1ˢᵗ Coming of the Church   of Jesus Christ   Throne Judgment

Church Age   Tribulation   Christ's Millennial Kingdom Eternity
(Unknown length)   (7 Years)   (1,000 years)   Future

Revelation 20:7, *"And when the thousand years are expired, Satan shall be loosed out of his prison, And shall go out to deceive the nations which are in the four quarters of the earth, Gog and Magog, to gather them together to battle: the number of whom is as the sand of the sea."*

At the end of the Millennium, Satan is going to be released from this Bottomless Pit, where he's been for

1,000 years, and he will try to gather up all the professors, not the possessors.

Remember, the people who entered into the Millennial Kingdom still living in their earthly bodies will be able to have children. Those children will be able to choose or reject Jesus Christ, the same choice that every other human being has to make.

If they reject Jesus Christ and his theocracy, after they are 100 years old, they will be accursed. As happens today, there will be those who will profess to believe in Jesus Christ, but have never truly done so. They profess faith in Christ, but they do not possess it.

Satan is released for this brief time so he can ferret out all of those professors, all of those nonbelievers. These will try to go against Jesus Christ in the city of Jerusalem, "the beloved city."

> Revelation 20:9-10, "*And they went up on the breadth of the earth, and compassed the camp of the saints about, and the beloved city: and fire came down from God out of heaven, and devoured them. And the devil that deceived them was cast into the lake of fire and brimstone, where the beast and the false prophet are, and shall be tormented day and night for ever and ever.*"

Satan will come to his ultimate end. Matthew 25:41 says that the fires of Hell were prepared for only Satan, Antichrist, the False Prophet, and all the evil angels that rebelled with Satan. It was never meant for humans. Those who choose to follow Satan instead of following Jesus will end up where Satan ends up. Satan is cast into his eternal damnation there in the Lake of Fire.

The Great White Throne Judgment

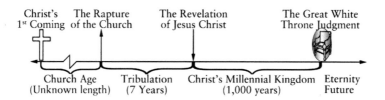

Now we come to a very sobering time as we look at the Great White Throne Judgment.

The Judge

> Revelation 20:11, *"And I saw a great white throne, and him that sat on it, from whose face the earth and the heaven fl ed away; and there was found no place for them."*

The Judge is going to be Jesus Christ. In John 5, we learn that God has given the task of judgment to His Son.

> John 5:22, *"For the Father judgeth no man, but hath committed all judgment unto the Son."*

And so the Judge at the Great White Throne Judgment is going to be Jesus Christ (Acts 10:42; 2 Timothy 4:1; 1 Peter 4:5).

The Judged

Revelation 20:15, *"And whosoever was not found written in the book of life was cast into the lake of fire."*

Now that is the judgment, but it also helps us to understand who will be judged. They will be those whose names are not written in the Book of Life. Some will have died, some will still be alive after the Millennial Kingdom, and they come now to the time when they are going to be judged for Eternity Future. The Bible refers to them all as "the dead" because they are spiritually dead.

Revelation 20:12-13, *"And I saw the dead, small and great, stand before God; and the books were opened: and another book was opened, which is the book of life: and the dead were judged out of those things which were written in the books, according to their works. And the sea gave up the dead which were in it; and death and hell delivered up the dead which were in them: and they were judged every man according to their works."*

There is the Bottomless Pit, Hell, and the Lake of Fire. I would suggest that they all have similar conditions but are three separate and distinct locations.

Hell here is the word from the Greek, "Hades." That's the location, the holding pen, for those who have rejected Jesus Christ. That's where they will have been sent. They've been there for maybe thousands of years awaiting the judgment, the sentencing. Think of Hell as jail, and the Lake of Fire as prison. Jail is temporary, prison is long term. Here we see the dead being released from Hell, only to be cast, forever, into the Lake of Fire.

A human judge will bring the accused in front of him where his guilt will be determined. If that individual is found guilty, that is the conclusion of one aspect of the trial. The prisoner is taken away to jail, to a holding pen. Later, the judge will bring the guilty party back for sentencing. And that is exactly what is taking place here. This judgment is not to decide whether a person is saved or lost; that will have already been determined for those who stand at the Great White Throne Judgment.

This is a judgment for those who have been awaiting their sentencing, those who had been in Hades waiting to be cast into the Lake of Fire.

Notice that there are "books" (plural), and another book. The book that is listed by itself is the Book of Life, which contains the names of those who have trusted Jesus Christ as Lord and Savior.

The books are the records of the sins that will have been committed by all of those who will be standing at the Great White Throne Judgment. There's going to be degrees of judgment for the lost, just as there will be degrees of rewards given out at the Judgment Seat of Christ to the saved. These books of the sins of these standing at the Great White Throne Judgment will be kept and a degree of punishment administered based upon what is found in these books.

The Judgment

The Bible talks about Hell delivering up those that are dead. Jesus Christ spoke more about Hell than He did Heaven – about 12 times more during His earthly ministry. Although we still do not know much about the place, we do know that Hell is the location where the fire is not quenched and their worm does not die (Mark 9).

This is an awesomely sobering study. Luke 16 describes Hell. I want to look at the conditions of Hell, the constraint of Hell, and the compassion that can be found there.

The conditions of Hell

First, I want to state that I do not believe that Luke 16 is a parable. Jesus Christ never explains it as a parable. In no other parable did Jesus use proper names; here He uses both Abraham and Lazarus. I believe it is a real event that took place and Jesus Christ just gives us this information so we can see what Hell is like.

Lazarus longed to take the crumbs that fell from the rich man's table while here on earth. Then death came.

Luke 16:22a, *"And it came to pass, that the beggar* [Lazarus] *died, and was carried by the angels into Abraham's bosom..."*

What a great thought! At death, angels will gather us up to take us into the presence of Jesus Christ.

170

Luke 16:22b-23a, *"the rich man also died, and was buried; And in hell he lift up his eyes, being in torments,"*

The first condition of Hell is torment; torment in the flame, burning where the fire is not quenched and their worm dies not.

I saw a friend of mine shortly after he had burned to death in a terrible accident. He was driving his gasoline truck down an old country road in south Georgia, when a farmer in a flatbed tractor pulled out into the path of his truck. The truck driver tried to avoid crashing into the farmer, but the truck rolled and gasoline spilled everywhere. My friend was burned to death. While I cannot describe the stench of burning flesh, I will never be able to forget it.

I thought, as we stood there looking at the wreckage, how it would have been just a few moments after he caught fire before death took him. If you could sustain the pain and agony that was touching his body at that point, that would be close to understanding the conditions of Hell.

Who would be foolish enough to purposefully turn on an eye of the stove to full heat, and then place their hand on the eye for 10 seconds. No one would, or should, ever do that – but if one did, one could begin to get some small idea of the first instant of being in Hell. The first condition of Hell is torment in the flame.

Luke 16:23b-24, *"and seeth Abraham afar off, and Lazarus in his bosom. And he cried and*

171

said, Father Abraham, have mercy on me, and send Lazarus, that he may dip the tip of his finger in water, and cool my tongue; for I am tormented in this flame."

The second condition of Hell is thirst. The rich man didn't ask for a gallon jug of water, a tea glass full of water, a coffee cup of water, or even for a teaspoon of water. He asked for a drop of water on the tip of a finger. But a drop would be more than he will ever be able to receive. Thirst that will never be relieved throughout all of eternity.

Luke 16:25, "But Abraham said, Son, remember that thou in thy lifetime receivedst thy good things, and likewise Lazarus evil things: but now he is comforted, and thou art tormented."

There is going to be thinking. He'll be able to remember. Torment, thirst, and thinking. Anybody going to Hell will think of every sermon they've ever heard, every Christian song they've ever heard, and every testimony they've ever been given. They will think about it forever. Terrible conditions.

The constraint of Hell

Luke 16:26, "And beside all this, between us and you there is a great gulf fixed: so that they which would pass from hence to you cannot; neither can they pass to us, that would come from thence."

The constraint of Hell is that there is no escape. Yes, as we talked about, Revelation 20 says that death and Hell will release those there to stand at the Great White Throne Judgment. But at that time, as they stand before Jesus Christ, they will be sentenced forever. They will all be condemned to the Lake of Fire. There is no escape. There is no end.

Can you imagine that? This rich man has been in Hell at least 2,000 years since the time of the events written in Luke 16. He'll continue to be there for the Millennial Kingdom, another 1,000 years. During all of that time, he is there in burning torment, thirst, and thinking. He cannot be released except to stand before Jesus Christ at the Great White Throne Judgment.

The rich man will step out of that awful place, only to stand before a God whom he has rejected, and to hear the words, "your name is not written in the Book of Life, sorry, I never knew you, depart from me." The man will start screaming and begging. Jesus Christ is compelled, because of the attributes of God, to cast him into the Lake of Fire where their worm dies not and the fire is not quenched.

My friend, this is a very sobering passage of Scripture found here in Revelation. Might I suggest you need to pray for those who do not know Jesus Christ, those loved ones, those friends, those close to you who need to know Jesus Christ.

Eternity Future

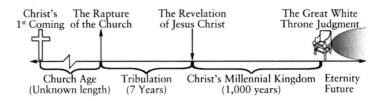

Now we come to the last two chapters of the book of Revelation. The sobering passage of Scripture we just studied is followed by Jesus Christ telling us that we are going to be on the victory side, and how it is going to be on into Eternity Future. The Great White Throne Judgment marks the end of history.

History had a beginning (Genesis 1:1, *"In the beginning...."*). It has been approximately 6,000 years since God created man until now, and there yet remains the 1,000 years of the Millennial Kingdom. So, for at least 7,000 years there will have been history.

However, at the beginning of the Great White Throne Judgment, history is concluded and we move into Eternity Future. In Eternity Future, there is going to be New Heavens, a New Earth, and a New Jerusalem. This teaching did not start in Revelation.

Isaiah 66:22, *"For as the new heavens and the new earth, which I will make, shall remain before me, saith the LORD, so shall your seed and your name remain."*

God is talking to the Jewish people and he gives them a promise. He introduces the New Heavens and the New Earth. As long as they will last – and they will last throughout eternity – so will the Jewish people remain as well.

> Isaiah 65:17, *"For, behold, I create new heavens and a new earth: and the former shall not be remembered, nor come into mind."*

This is not refurbishing the old earth, this is bringing a New Earth into existence. It's going to be so beautiful, these New Heavens and this New Earth; we are not even going to think about the old earth.

> Isaiah 65:18-19, *"But be ye glad and rejoice for ever in that which I create: for, behold, I create Jerusalem a rejoicing, and her people a joy. And I will rejoice in Jerusalem, and joy in my people: and the voice of weeping shall be no more heard in her, nor the voice of crying."*

What a time it's going to be! The New Heavens and the New Earth in Eternity Future.

On this New Earth there is going to be a city of Jerusalem. But, there's going to be two different Jerusalems in the future: a Jerusalem on the earth and a New Jerusalem hanging in outer space.

In the Abrahamic covenant (Genesis 15:18-21), God told Abraham he would give his people the descendants of Abraham, the Jewish people, a section of real estate over in the Middle East, which approximately is 10 times the size of the land that they have today.

According to the 38 passages of Scripture that deal with the Biblical borders of Israel, the actual Promised Land includes what we know as half of Egypt, all of Israel, all of Lebanon, all of Syria, all of Jordan, three-quarters of Iraq, three-quarters of Saudi Arabia, and all of Kuwait.

Maybe now you can understand the problem over in the Middle East. Those who are not Jewish realize what God is ultimately going to do. In fact, the late president of Syria said the problem in the Middle East is that these Jews believe the Bible. They believe God is going to give them all this land. That is indeed the case and, in the Millennial Kingdom, they will have that land.

On the New Earth in Eternity Future, they will have that land as well because God said I will give it to you forever, olam, as long as God is. His eternality is applied to the promise that was given to Abraham, Isaac, and Jacob for the Jewish people about the land that they shall have forever.

The New Jerusalem

There is a description of the New Jerusalem and again, I'm just going to touch the surface with what is going to be there.

Revelation 21:10-12, 21, *"And he carried me away in the spirit to a great and high mountain,*

*and shewed me that great city, the holy Jerusa-
lem, descending out of heaven from God, Having the glory of God: and her light was like unto
a stone most precious, even like a jasper stone,
clear as crystal; And had a wall great and high,
and had twelve gates, and at the gates twelve
angels, and names written thereon, which are
the names of the twelve tribes of the children of
Israel:... And the twelve gates were twelve
pearls; every several gate was of one pearl: and
the street of the city was pure gold, as it were
transparent glass."*

The names of the 12 tribes of the children of Israel
on the gates allows each tribe to enter by their own
gate. The Jewish people will be on the earth. Remember, the New Jerusalem will not be on earth, but hovering in space like the moon. Next time you look at the
moon from your vantage point here on earth, you'll
understand what I'm talking about.

Let me show you why I make that statement.

Revelation 21:22, *"And I saw no temple therein:
for the Lord God Almighty and the Lamb are
the temple of it."*

In other words, God and Jesus Christ will be in the
New Jerusalem, thus there is no need for a Temple.

Ezekiel 37:26-28 says there will be a Temple forever
on the Temple Mount in Jerusalem. The Bible does not
contradict itself. Therefore, we cannot assume that the
New Jerusalem will be on earth. In fact, we have to as-

sume the opposite. It will be hanging in space; it will be separate from the New Earth.

The Jerusalem where Jesus Christ will rule and reign among the Jews, dwelling, inhabiting Himself among His people, the Jewish people and the Gentiles who are believers, who come through the Millennial Kingdom, who enter into the Eternity Future, they are given this piece of real estate promised and indeed they will come to worship in Jerusalem.

The Bible says the feast of tabernacles will be worshipped throughout Eternity Future (Zechariah 14). The New Jerusalem is going to be hovering in the heavens.

By the way, there are not "streets" in the New Jerusalem. We will not be walking on "streets of gold."

> Revelation 21:21, "*And the twelve gates were twelve pearls; every several gate was of one pearl: and the street of the city was pure gold, as it were transparent glass.*"

There is just one street, not multiple streets.

> Revelation 22:2, "*In the midst of the street of it, and on either side of the river, was there the tree of life, which bare twelve manner of fruits, and yielded her fruit every month: and the leaves of the tree were for the healing of the nations.*"

There is only one street in the New Jerusalem. What does that mean? We all live on Main Street. Nobody will live on a side street in downtown Jerusalem; the

New Jerusalem, that is, is where we live in Eternity Future.

There is so, so much here. I hope that you will study these two chapters and come to a better understanding of the New Heavens, the New Earth, and the New Jerusalem.

We'll have access to the earth. We'll be able to come back to the earth, and the Jews and the Gentiles on earth will have access to the New Jerusalem; the Jews in particular entering through that gate which has their name on it, the name of their tribe. The habitation for Eternity Future will be the earth for the Gentiles and the Jews and the New Jerusalem for the Christians, the body of Christ, the bride of Jesus Christ. What a time it's going to be!

John the Apostle received all of this information. He was overwhelmed. He just could not believe what he had heard, but he had to write it down. The Lord told him to write it all down and send it to us and what a blessing it is that he sent this information to us. We could spend many, many more hours in this study. And I am hoping and praying that that is exactly what you're going to do as you study the book of Revelation.

Conclusion

Jesus Christ says to John, write this down for everybody to read.

Revelation 22:7, *"Behold, I come quickly: blessed is he that keepeth the sayings of the prophecy of this book."*

That's how we are to live. We are to live by studying this book and keeping the sayings. Do what He has told us to do in his only way of communicating to us – through His Word.

Revelation 22:12, *"And, behold, I come quickly; and my reward is with me, to give every man according as his work shall be."*

That's why we live this way, that's why we live by the book. Jesus Christ is coming to give us our reward and, thus, we live in light of receiving those rewards. Remember in Revelation 4:10, we take all the rewards we receive from Him, we take them to the foot of the throne, we cast them before Him in thanksgiving for what He has done.

"Behold, I come quickly and blessed is he that keeps the sayings of this book" – that's how we should live. "Behold I come quickly and my reward is with me" – that's why we live that way. Look at the response of John the Apostle who wrote the book of Revelation.

Revelation 22:20, *"He which testifieth these things saith, Surely I come quickly. Amen. Even so, come, Lord Jesus."*

We know how to live, we know why to live; and now he says he is coming quickly. What was John's response after writing down the entire book of Revelation, all of this unbelievable prophecy that God gave him to pass along to us? His prayer was, "Even so, come, Lord Jesus."

Is that your prayer? Are your priorities right? Are you looking for the return of Jesus Christ? Do you eagerly anticipate with great joy that it may happen at any moment? Is that what you would like to have happen?

"Even so, come, Lord Jesus." That is my prayer on a daily basis. Now, that prayer has not been answered for some 2,000 years, but it will be answered. I believe it will be answered in the very near future.

If you are not a Christian, how can you prepare for the Lord's return? Getting prepared is as simple as A,B,C.

"A", admit that you are a sinner in need of a Saviour to take away your sin.

"B", believe that Jesus Christ died for you to take away that sin. Believe that He rose from the dead to prove He is who He said He is and can do what He said He would do. Believe that He will save you as He said He would.

"C", call upon Him to save you. The Bible says in Romans 10:13, "whosoever shall call upon the name of the Lord shall be saved."

I believe Jesus Christ is coming very soon. The Rapture of the Church could take place at any moment! That truth should cause all of us to want to live pure and be productive in light of what seems to be a soon return of Jesus Christ. Having said that, there is nothing left for me to say after this study except let's keep looking up... Until.

Revelation: A Chronology   Dr. Jimmy DeYoung

Revelation: A Chronology

Dr. Jimmy DeYoung

APPENDICES

Here are some additional quick-reference charts and study aids to help you develop your understanding of the book of Revelation, and Bible prophecy as a whole.

Chart: The Sets of Judgments Compared

	Seals *Revelation 5-6*	Trumpets *Revelation 8-9*	Vials *Revelation 16*
1	Rider on a White Horse - Antichrist	One-third of the earth burned	Plague of terrible sores
2	Rider on a Red Horse - War	One-third of all sea creatures die	Sea turns to blood, all sea life dies
3	Rider on a Black Horse - Famine	Stars fall; one-third of water turns bitter	Rivers to blood, all water life dies
4	Rider on a Pale Horse - Death	One-third sun, moon, and stars darkened	The sun scorches the earth
5	Martyrdom	Woes, Abaddon, locusts	Beast's kingdom is darkened
6	Signs in the sky, earthquakes, nature	One-third of people killed by horsemen	The Euphrates River runs dry
7	Silence, Trumpets begin	Wrath / Reward	Babylon is destroyed

Chart: Dreams from Daniel

Dream of Nebuchadnezzar	Gentile Power	Dream of Daniel
Head of Gold	Babylonian Empire	Lion with Eagle's Wings
Chest and Arms of Silver	Medo-Persian Empire	Bear with Three Ribs in its Mouth
Waist and Thighs of Brass	Grecian Empire	Leopard with Four Heads and Four Wings
Legs of Iron	Roman Empire	Dreadful Beast with 10 Horns
Feet of Iron and Clay	Revived Roman Empire	The Little Horn

Scripture Index

Subject Index

About Jimmy DeYoung

Jimmy DeYoung is a prophecy teacher and journalist who travels the country and the world educating the Body of Christ of the future events foretold in God's prophetic Word.

His goal is to equip Christians with the knowledge and understanding of what God's Word says will happen someday soon, so that they can make better decisions today.

Jimmy DeYoung has several ministries to this end: Prophecy Today Radio, the School of Prophets, the Until Newsletter, Shofar Communications, Joshua Travel, and more. Here are a few of his websites:

www.jimmydeyoung.com

www.prophecytoday.com

www.schoolofprophets.org

www.prophecybookstore.com

www.joshuatravel.com

Jimmy DeYoung and his wife of over 50 years, Judy, resided in Jerusalem for 12 years, where he held full credentials as a journalist in the second most populated journalistic city in the world. Arriving there just 3 days prior to the Gulf Crisis in 1991, he weathered 39 Scud attacks. Jimmy gave reports nationwide on several networks during the Gulf Crisis. Today he continues to have his finger on the pulse of what is considered the media "hot spot" of our time, the Middle East. On his travels throughout the U.S. and around the world, Jimmy brings with him the latest news from out of the Middle East with a unique blend of political, Biblical, and prophetic insight that cannot be found in the media today.

After graduating from Tennessee Temple University in Chattanooga, Tennessee, Jimmy joined with Jack Wyrtzen and Harry Bollback at Word of Life Fellowship in Schroon Lake, New York. There he spent the next twelve years in many staff positions, including staff evangelist, host of Word of Life Inn, and producer of radio programs heard worldwide.

For the next 5 years Jimmy was the Vice-President and General Manager of New York City's first Christian radio station, WNYM. During his time at the station, Jimmy was the producer and host of a daily talk program in the #1 media market in America.

Upon first arriving in Israel, moved by the plight of the Israeli people and by the spirit of God, Dr. DeYoung founded the Assembly at Jerusalem, a Bible-preaching church that meets in the holy city. Today, Jimmy travels the world proclaiming the good news of Christ's gift of eternal life and soon coming return for His Church, using the means of media, radio, television, books, and the internet, as well as by preaching in churches and assemblies across the globe.

Jimmy has met and interviewed many international leaders including: Prime Minister Benjamin Netanyahu, former Prime Minister Ariel Sharon, former Israeli Foreign Minister Shimon Peres, former Prime Minister

Ehud Olmert, former Israeli Defense Minister Moshe
Arens, Jordan's Foreign Minister Marwan Muasher,
and the late Palestinian leader Yasser Arafat.

Jimmy is seen on the *Day of Discovery* television
program, which is produced in the Middle East, and is
a frequent guest on *the John Ankerberg Show*. He is
also heard daily and weekly on radio and internet, with
the latest reports from the Middle East on several networks consisting of over 1,500 stations.

Jimmy is a noted conference speaker in the United
States, Europe, and South America, and he devotes several months out of each year to this conference sched-
ule. He has authored the best selling book, *Sound The
Trumpets*, co-authored *Israeli Under Fire* with Dr. John
Ankerberg, produced a number of audio and video materials, including his best seller, *Ready To Rebuild*, a
documentary on the building of the Third Temple.
Jimmy continues to monitor the most current events as
they unfold in the Middle East and compares these current events to the prophetic truth of God's Word.

Jimmy had the privilege of receiving his Doctorate
from Tennessee Temple University in May of 1996. He
also received his Ph.D. from Louisiana Baptist University in May of 2000.

The School of Prophets

Jimmy has a deep desire to have as many people in
the Body of Christ to understand Bible prophecy, which
makes up one-third of the God's Word. To that end, he

started the *School of Prophets* in partnership with Louisiana Baptist University, which offers both a Masters (MA) Degree and a Doctoral (PhD) Degree in Advanced Prophetics.

The courses provided at the School of Prophets are derived from Jimmy DeYoung's study of the Bible and he is integrally involved in the school. Jimmy grades papers, evaluates projects and provides specific feedback to each individual throughout the entire program.

If you are interested in this exhaustive and systematic graduate-level study of Bible prophecy, please visit www.schoolofprophets.org.

LaVergne, TN USA
17 January 2011
212809LV00002B/2/P